D1621217

Shakespeare's CHURCH

A PARISH FOR THE WORLD

THE GRAVE
OF THE POET
WILLIAM
SHAKESPEARE

Shakespeare's CHURCH

A PARISH FOR THE WORLD

Written and edited by Val Horsler

With the Revd Martin Gorick and Dr Paul Edmondson

Introduction by Professor Jonathan Bate

Endorsed by The Shakespeare Birthplace Trust www.shakespeare.org.uk

First published in 2010 by
Third Millennium Publishing Limited, a subsidiary of Third Millennium Information Limited

2–5 Benjamin Street
London
United Kingdom
EC1M 5QL
www.tmiltd.com

ISBN 978 1 906507 33 6

British Library Cataloguing in Publication Data
A CIP catalogue record for this book is available from the British Library.

Edited by Val Horsler
Designed by Helen Swansbourne
Production by Bonnie Murray
Printed by Scotprint in Scotland

Jacket front: Shakespeare's monument in the sanctuary
Jacket back: Pre-Reformation glass in the north-east chancel window
Frontispiece: The sanctuary
Endpapers: Perpendicular architecture in the nave

Picture credits
Julian Andrews frontispiece, 88–89, 91, 93, 127, 128 *tr, cr, br*, 129, 130–131, 133; John Cheal endpapers, 5, 10, 11, 12, 13, 15, 25*t*, 35*t*, 36*b*, 39*t*, 40*l*, 42*l*, 43, 48*b*, 49, 56, 63*r*, 65, 67*b*, 72, 74, 79, 80, 84*b*, 85, 87, 102, 103, 105, 113, 115, 117, 121, 135, 138*t*, 139, 148–9, 150, 151, 152, 153; Sarah Douglas 128*tl*; Michael Dyer 155; Roy Fox 7, 30–31, 36*t*, 37, 38, 39 *bl, bc, br*, 41, 44, 45*r*, 46, 47, 48*t*, 50, 51, 52, 53, 55, 57, 58, 59*r*, 60, 61*b*, 62, 63*l*, 67*t*, 68, 69, 70, 71, 73, 77, 78, 106–107, 109, 110, 112, 119*t*, 122, 123; Martin Gorick 18*tl*, 32*b*, 34, 147; Bill Hicks 84*t*; Felicity Howlett 40*r*, 137*t*, 143*tr*; Ann Lawson 132; Harry Lomax 8, 16–17, 33, 42*r*, 61*t*, 64, 134; Esther Naylor 19, 75, back jacket; Tim Raistrick 136*l*, 137*b*, 142*b*; Royal Shakespeare Company 141*b*; Ursula Russell 142*t*, 143*l*, *bl*; The Shakespeare Birthplace Trust 18*b*, 20, 21, 22, 27, 28, 54*b*, 66*l*, 76, 81, 82, 83, 90*b*, 94*t*, 95*t*, 96, 97, 98–9, 99, 101, 111, 118, 120, 124, 125, 136*r*, 138*b*, 140, 141*t*; John McKenzie 144, 145; Simon Wilding 25*b*, 32*t*, 45*l*, 54*t*, 59*l*, 66*r*, 86, 90*t*, 108, 116, 119*b*. Pen-and-ink sketches by Gerald E Moira, from *Shakespeare's True Life* by James Walter, 1890

Acknowledgements

Grateful acknowledgement is made to The Hosking Houses Trust for the Residency August 2009. www.hoskinghouses.co.uk

The quotations from Shakespeare's work in the main text are from William Shakespeare, *The Complete Works*, edited by Stanley Wells and Gary Taylor, with John Jowett and William Montgomery, 2nd edition (Oxford: Clarendon Press, 2004). Those in the Introduction are from *The RSC Shakespeare: Complete Works*, edited by Jonathan Bate and Eric Rasmussen (Macmillan, 2007). The quotation from *The Diary of Virginia Woolf*, edited by Anne Olivier Bell, published by Hogarth Press, is reprinted by permission of The Random House Group Ltd; and that from Ursula Bloom's *Rosemary for Stratford-on-Avon* is copyright Ursula Bloom literary estate. Spellings throughout have been modernised except those directly transcribed from inscriptions. A short Glossary is provided to explain terms and phrases that may be unfamiliar.

Huge thanks are due to the many members of the staff and parishioners of Holy Trinity church who gave unstintingly of their time and expertise in showing the author around the church and then in reading, commenting on and contributing to the text: Bill Hicks on the Cloptons, the heraldry and the building generally; Tony Boyd-Williams and Ursula Russell on the drama; Harry Lomax and Felicity Howlett with their photographs; Sir Brian Follett and Jo Walker on the Friends of Shakespeare's Church; Will Hawkes on the kneelers; Andrew Jones on the music; Freda Kitcher on the history; Jon Ormrod and Sheonagh Ormrod on spirituality and drama; Ronnie Mulryne on the history of the church, guild and school; Tim Raistrick on the choir and much else; Margaret Sweet on her long connection with the church; Charles Wilson on the bells; and Nigel Penn and Nigel Wyatt with their general helpfulness and knowledge. Special thanks go to John Cheal for his splendidly perceptive photographs.

Members of staff at The Shakespeare Birthplace Trust (which is endorsing this publication) were equally generous with their time, their contributions and their detailed comments: Robert Bearman and Mairi Macdonald with their huge knowledge of the archives, freely shared; Professor Stanley Wells on Shakespeare himself; and Susan Walker with the educational material.

Diana Price kindly gave permission for her article on Shakespeare's monument to be used, and Professor Jonathan Bate not only read and commented on the text but contributed the Introduction. John Barnard assisted with the Keats connection. We are thrilled that Dame Judi Dench wrote the Preface. All of the historical pictures are from the collections of The Shakespeare Birthplace Trust, open through the year: www.shakespeare.org.uk

As ever, it was a pleasure to work with the highly professional and committed staff of Third Millennium Publishing, from the chairman Julian Platt, to the publisher Chris Fagg, the production manager Bonnie Murray, the marketing manager Michael Jackson and the designer Helen Swansbourne, as well as Matt Wilson, Joel Burden, Neil Burkey and Phil Reid.

CONTENTS

PREFACE

It's extraordinary to think that the church that houses the grave of the world's greatest dramatist will reach its 800th anniversary in 2010. Holy Trinity Church, Stratford-upon-Avon has been the linchpin of its community for all that time, and continues to be so. Indeed I've always loved to spend time there myself whenever I've been playing in Stratford. Yet with all its history, Shakespeare's church needs substantial funds to maintain it as a place of pilgrimage for over 200,000 visitors a year, and as a focus for a global community of Shakespeare lovers.

To celebrate its anniversary, Holy Trinity Church has joined with Third Millennium Publishing to produce a celebratory volume – and this is the result: a richly illustrated, beautifully designed and produced volume to treasure. For every book sold, a royalty goes to the Friends of Shakespeare's Church which will be added to the restoration funds which will help keep this church alive for the pleasure and spiritual comfort of future generations to come.

Judi Dench

DAME JUDI DENCH

INTRODUCTION: SHAKESPEARE'S STRATFORD

Jonathan Bate, Professor of Shakespeare and Renaissance Literature at the University of Warwick

William Shakespeare's bones lie in Holy Trinity Church. As you will see in the beautifully illustrated book you are about to read, his monument is there on the wall: 'IVDICIO PYLIUM, GENIO SOCRATEM, ARTE MARONEM, / TERRA TEGIT, POPULUS MAERET, OLYMPUS HABET.' 'A Pylus in judgement, a Socrates in genius, a Maro in art, / The earth buries him, the people mourn him, Olympus possesses him.' A man with the judgement of Nestor, King of Pylus, wisest of the ancient Greeks at Troy; with the talent of Socrates, greatest of philosophers; and with the literary art of Virgil (Publius Virgilius Maro), who was regarded in Shakespeare's time as the greatest poet in history. 'His body is beneath the earth', the inscription continues – it is here, that is to say, in Holy Trinity – and his loss is 'mourned by the people'. As a man of the theatre he was indeed a *popular* poet. But the place to which he has gone is Mount Olympus, the home of the gods. This was as if to say that his was truly an Olympian genius. Though one does wonder whether the author of the memorial lines – possibly Shakespeare's son-in-law John Hall or even his clever daughter Susanna – might have muddled up Mount Olympus with Mount Parnassus, the traditional home of the Muses.

Then beneath the Latin inscription, there is an English one claiming that nature herself died with Shakespeare, the point being that more than any other writer he had succeeded in answering to what his most famous creation, Hamlet Prince of Denmark, calls 'the purpose of playing': 'to hold, as 'twere, the mirror up to nature'. But despair not, passerby: his writings survive as vessels of his 'living art'.

Those strange people – conspiracy theorists to a man – who do not believe that Shakespeare wrote Shakespeare have a way of dismissing sixteenth-century Stratford-upon-Avon as a provincial backwater. As is amply shown in the book you are holding, this was far from the case. The very eloquence and Latinity of Shakespeare's own monument is testament enough in itself: it shows that his own town held relatives and friends who knew his work and knew that it was good.

Holy Trinity matters to those who love and admire Shakespeare not only because his physical remains are there. It was also a fixed point in his life. Every day when he went into his garden at New Place (perhaps to check on his mulberry tree), he saw the tower of the church pointing his thoughts to heaven. The first record of his life places him in the church: he was baptised there on April 26 1564.

What kind of a place was the Stratford into which the boy was born? A crossroads between old and new worlds: to the north, the ancient forest of Arden; to the south, rich farming land, then, beyond, the university city of Oxford. To the east, Kenilworth Castle, home of Queen Elizabeth's sometime favourite, Robert Dudley, Earl of Leicester, and just beyond that, the great city of Coventry, the fourth largest city in the land, where the old Biblical plays from medieval times – Creation and Flood, Crucifixion and Judgment – were still performed every year on pageant carts stationed around the city.

Queen Elizabeth I has been on the throne for six years. We're at the beginning of the fabled Elizabethan age. The

English language is exploding with new vocabulary, intellectual life is fizzing with new ideas and England is beginning to become a great nation. But here in the peace of the countryside, the old stories and customs live on. Here fairies and hobgoblins are real – and dangerous. When the fairies are angry:

> The ploughman lost his sweat, and the green corn
> Hath rotted ere his youth attained a beard.
> The fold stands empty in the drownèd field,
> And crows are fatted with the murrion flock,
> The nine men's morris is filled up with mud,
> And the quaint mazes in the wanton green
> For lack of tread are undistinguishable.
>
> (*A Midsummer Night's Dream*)

And at night they can get up to all sorts of mischief:

> O, then I see Queen Mab hath been with you:
> She is the fairies' midwife, and she comes
> In shape no bigger than an agate-stone
> On the forefinger of an alderman,
> Drawn with a team of little atomies
> Over men's noses as they lie asleep.
>
> (*Romeo and Juliet*)

The forefinger of an alderman: that's John Shakespeare, town councillor, the boy William's father.

It was a sleepy little town, Stratford, with its population of 1500, but it came to life once a week on market days. Farmers came in from the surrounding villages with their livestock, crossing the Avon via the Clopton Bridge, then up Sheep Street to the Market Cross. The narrow streets were crowded: John Shakespeare was fined for not clearing the dunghill from the front of his house on Henley Street. That's the Stratford into which William Shakespeare was born.

A mere two months into his life, Stratford was hit by a terrible outbreak of plague. Nearly a quarter of the town was wiped out. The Shakespeares were lucky to escape unscathed. They had already lost two children; little William was the first child in the family to survive. A boy, at that. If his arrival was the cause of great joy, his survival must have seemed like a miracle. An heir, a vouchsafe of immortality: 'This were to be new made when thou art old / And see thy blood warm when thou feel'st it cold' (Sonnet 15). Soon there would be other brothers and a sister for William: Joan, Gilbert, Richard and finally young Edmund. But it was with William that the Shakespeares became a family.

In the year of the child's birth, the paterfamilias, John Shakespeare, had much on his mind. His glove-making business was going well. He was dealing (illegally) in wool on the side. And he was beginning to create an impression in local government. He started as a petty official dealing with complaints about false measures and watered ale; by now he had graduated to chamberlain, keeper of the town's accounts. Eventually he would become bailiff, in effect the mayor of Stratford-upon-Avon. A person of some significance – until he fell into debt and stopped attending council meetings, even stopped going to church.

In the winter of 1564, six months after William's birth, he added a new entry in the chamberlain's accounts: 'Item, the sum of two shillings, paid for defacing images.' These were dramatic times. For centuries out of memory prayers for the souls of the Stratford departed had been said in the Guild Chapel next door to the school on the corner of Church Street and Dead Lane. The congregation marvelled at its walls covered in brightly painted frescoes, in red and gold, argent and ochre. You would have seen St George slay the dragon, St Thomas à Becket fall to his murderers' swords, Christ rise from the tomb and all scores settled at the Last Judgment. Not any more. With the Protestant revolution, Purgatory was abolished at a stroke and prayers for the dead became redundant. As for the images, the Bible was quite clear. 'Thou shalt not make thee any graven image, or any likeness of anything that is in heaven above, or that is in the earth beneath, or that is in the waves beneath the earth.' So John Shakespeare paid those two shillings to the workmen who, with buckets of whitewash, assiduously covered over all these images, obliterating the signs of a shared faith and a folk memory.

All this was very new. It was only thirty years before – within John Shakespeare's lifetime – that Henry VIII had defied the Pope over his divorce and broken from the Roman Catholic faith which had held sway in Britain for a thousand years, summarily shattering the religious unity of Europe. The Church of England was born and the new theology of the Reformation ruthlessly imposed. Statues were smashed up, the monasteries were torn down, their ruins scattered across the shires like so many broken teeth:

> When I have seen by Time's fell hand defaced
> The rich-proud cost of outworn buried age,
> When sometime lofty towers I see down-razed
> And brass eternal slave to mortal rage.
>
> (Sonnet 64)

The brutal enforcers of the Protestant hard line stalked the land like some Tudor Taliban. Communities were divided. As a prominent member of the strongly Protestant Stratford Corporation John was expected to bring up his son and heir William to be a god-fearing Anglican. Perhaps he did – or perhaps, like many others, he secretly remained loyal to the old faith.

William's mother Mary was an Arden, connected by name to one of the most prosperous and respectable Roman Catholic families in the predominantly Roman Catholic region of Warwickshire. But no one was safe. Being a Papist was a dangerous business. The dreaded Francis Walsingham, head of the Queen's Secret Police, had his tentacles everywhere. If you were found out hiding a Catholic priest, you could be charged with treason and beheaded. Where Shakespeare came from, safety meant keeping your head down, holding the cards of your own beliefs close to your chest. He had every reason to grow up being discreet.

Throughout his career in the London theatre, which began around 1590 when he was in his mid-twenties, he kept going back to Stratford. While his fellow-actors bought big houses in nice suburbs such as Dulwich and Fulham, Shakespeare never felt part of the London scene. He rented cheap rooms, he stayed on the move. Even the taxman had difficulty keeping up with his changes of address. Paying taxes at the last possible minute: maintaining the great traditions of the theatre.

He spent his money on property and land in his home town. New Place, the second-biggest house in town. Five gables and a gentleman's coat-of-arms over the door. He bought meadows and barns and grain-stores; he speculated on the agricultural commodities market and built up a buy-to-let property portfolio. A family home, a gentleman's status to make up for his father's financial disgrace, a loyal wife, investment income: by the time that Queen Elizabeth died and King James came to the throne in 1603, he seemed to have everything.

But perhaps the most important thing of all was missing. The Parish Register, Stratford-upon-Avon, 1596, August 11, Buried, Hamnet filius William Shakspere. Judith's twin. His

He was growing prematurely bald. He was growing old. He raged more and more against Time:

> That time of year thou mayst in me behold
> When yellow leaves, or none, or few, do hang
> Upon those boughs which shake against the cold,
> Bare ruined choirs, where late the sweet birds sang.
> In me thou seest the twilight of such day
> As after sunset fadeth in the west,
> Which by and by black night doth take away,
> Death's second self, that seals up all in rest.
> In me thou seest the glowing of such fire
> That on the ashes of his youth doth lie,
> As the death-bed whereon it must expire,
> Consumed with that which it was nourished by.
> This thou perceiv'st, which makes thy love more strong,
> To love that well which thou must leave ere long.
>
> (Sonnet 73)

only son and heir, aged just eleven, dead, at the very moment that Shakespeare's plays were triumphing on the London stage:

> Never, never
> Must I behold my pretty baby more…
> Grief fills the room up of my absent child:
> Lies in his bed, walks up and down with me,
> Puts on his pretty looks, repeats his words,
> Remembers me of all his gracious parts,
> Stuffs out his vacant garments with his form.
>
> (*King John*)

Times were tough in the theatre world during the early years of King James's reign – extended outbreaks of plague meant that the playhouses were kept closed for months and months at a time. The actors had to go on the road to earn their keep. Shakespeare was financially secure by now, and no longer had the appetite for the hardships of touring. Bed and board in provincial towns. Packing costumes and props into carts, then moving on. No, he spent more and more time back home in Stratford. He went on writing plays, but at a much slower rate than before, often in collaboration with others.

We can be confident that he worshipped in Holy Trinity on many a Sunday. It is often supposed that Shakespeare spent very little time in Stratford between the late 1580s, when he left to begin his theatre career in London, and his last five years, but this supposition is not supported by the evidence. Between 1604 and 1611, all the firm documentary records of Shakespeare place him in Stratford. He was often to be seen in the local courts, involved in disputes over money and property transactions. In 1612 he was back in London, acting as witness in a law case involving a former landlord. There he is described as 'William Shakespeare of Stratford-upon-Avon in the county of Warwick, gentleman, of the age of forty-eight or thereabouts'. He is not identified, then, by means of his connection with the rackety London theatre world: he has attained gentility and settled back in his home.

As his fellow-actors, now called the King's Men, proudly played in front of the royal family, Shakespeare was in his forties with two grown daughters. In 1607, Susanna, twenty-five years old, married John Hall. Her husband was a doctor: just what every father wants for his eldest daughter. She soon gave birth to a girl, Elizabeth, Shakespeare's first grandchild – the only grandchild he would know. 'Now, mild may be thy life,' says Pericles to his baby daughter in the play that Shakespeare was working on at the time:

> For a more blusterous birth had never babe.
> Quiet and gentle thy conditions, for
> Thou art the rudeliest welcome to this world
> That ever was prince's child.
>
> (*Pericles*)

From things dying to things newborn. The loss of Hamnet was partially redeemed. Shakespeare started writing a sequence of romances full of strange adventures, of magic, of children lost and found, of new life.

The ageing playwright kept one foot in London. He bought a gatehouse in Blackfriars, close by his company's new indoor playhouse. He co-scripted three plays with young John Fletcher, who was filling his shoes as resident dramatist for the King's Men. But most of the time now, he was at home in Stratford. Looking after his house and land. Playing another part: that of a respectable country gentleman. They tried to draw him into a dispute over the enclosure of common land on the Welcombe Hills just outside town. But he kept his counsel. 'My cousin Shakespeare', noted a kinsman in his diary, 'says he thinks there will be nothing done at all.'

He read Montaigne, he thought about death, he cultivated his garden:

> O, you heavenly charmers,
> What things you make of us! For what we lack
> We laugh, for what we have are sorry, still
> Are children in some kind. Let us be thankful
> For that which is, and with you leave dispute
> That are above our question. Let's go off,
> And bear us like the time.
>
> (*The Two Noble Kinsmen*)

The last words that Shakespeare ever wrote for the stage, as Duke Theseus leads the company to a wedding – but before it, a funeral. William Shakespeare was buried in Holy Trinity on April 25 1616, the day before the fifty-second anniversary of his baptism.

Warwick 2010

HOLY TRINITY: EIGHT CENTURIES OF SERVICE

The Collegiate Church of the Holy and Undivided Trinity has been for at least 800 years the place where the people of Stratford-upon-Avon have come to worship; the earliest part of the present building dates to around 1210 and is Stratford's oldest building. And because it is also the burial place of William Shakespeare, regarded by many as the greatest poet and playwright of all time, it welcomes many more thousands of visitors every year who come to pay homage to the great man and to wonder at the inscription on his grave. Many of them also use their time in the church to light a candle and to pray, hence the sub-title of this book: 'A parish for the world'.

Holy Trinity's history goes back much further than the earliest fabric of the current structure; there was certainly a place of worship on this site by the eighth century AD. And it is much more than Shakespeare's resting place: the Clopton tomb in the north aisle is regarded by many experts as one of the finest Renaissance monuments in Europe; and the fine carving on the fifteenth-century misericords in the chancel bears witness not just to superb craftsmanship but also to the social life of 600 years ago. If you know where to look, there are all sorts of fascinating testaments to the church's venerable history and the many changes in beliefs and patterns of worship that it has witnessed.

It is also a vigorous, living church, playing a central part in the life of its town. People come here not just to worship, or for baptisms, weddings and funerals, but to play music and sing in the choir, and to take part in dramatic productions; schoolchildren dress up as their Elizabethan forebears and find out what it was like to be a child living in Stratford 400 years ago; and bell-ringers summon the faithful to prayer just as they did in Shakespeare's time. He would find many differences if he were to come back to Holy Trinity today, but he would also find a great deal that he would recognise – not least a church clearly at the centre of a vibrant Christian community.

It is that church that this book celebrates, both for the millions who know it and visit it mainly for its famous resident and for the thousands for whom, whether they are townspeople or not, it echoes with a ringing and living Christian faith.

So long as men can breathe or eyes can see,
So long lives this, and this gives life to thee.

(SONNET 18)

HISTORY OF THE CHURCH

Shall we go see the relics of this town?

(*TWELFTH NIGHT, OR WHAT YOU WILL*, 3.3)

ANGLO-SAXON ORIGINS

Holy Trinity church sits on a raised piece of land close to the bank of the River Avon – an ideal site for ease of transport and communication when these were vital elements in the placing of settlements. Not only was there a river to provide a thoroughfare, but there was a ford nearby too, dating back to Roman times, to allow the river to be crossed. Flooding was an ever-present danger, as it still is, particularly on the floodplain on the opposite bank, but the slight hill on which the church stands provides a degree of safety. And the power of the water could be diverted into the millrace at Lucy's Mill, mentioned in Domesday Book and still existing downstream from the church.

Above left: View from the spire.

Below: View from Cross o' the Hill, 1746.

Opposite: Pre-Reformation glass in the north-east chancel window.

THE SOUTH EAST VIEW OF Stratford Church Dedicated to the HOLY TRINITY

John Jordan's view of Holy Trinity, *c* 1790.

Sometime in the eighth century AD the land here became part of the newly established See of Worcester, a link which survived until 1919 when authority was transferred to the diocese of Coventry. The first reliable record of a place of worship comes in a charter of AD 845 signed by Beorthwulf, King of Mercia, granting privileges to the monks who lived here: 'that they may be free for ever from all bondage and service, all taxes and imposts, whether in field or wood, mead or pasture, river or fishery, that they shall not be called on to find refreshment for king or noble, even when hunting or hawking'. These rights were to be theirs 'so long as the Christian faith shall last among the Angles in Britain'.

The first building is likely to have been of wood which, in common with many other English churches and cathedrals, may have been replaced in stone after the Norman invasion. The Domesday Book of 1086 records that the Bishop of Worcester's holdings here were valuable – then worth £25 in contrast to its value under Edward the Confessor of only 100s (£5) – and mentions 'fourteen and a half hides of land' (about 2000 acres) and 'twenty-one villeins and a priest', as well as 'a mill yielding ten shillings and 1000 eels'. There was presumably some kind of chapel where the priest would have said Mass, but earlier buildings almost certainly stood where the current church stands, which means that all memory of them has been swallowed up within the later rebuildings – though there are some tantalising ghosts. The door in the north wall of the chancel, which is now blocked up and leads nowhere, once opened into a building outside, the basement of which was later used as a charnel house; chroniclers who knew it before it was demolished in 1800 believed that it was possibly part of an early church. And still to be seen today, on the undersides of a few of the stone steps that wind up to the bell chamber behind the little door in the south-east corner of the crossing, are traces of carving which indicate that these steps are likely to be reused parts of the earlier church, or perhaps its gravestones.

The fortunes of Stratford itself, situated on its advantageous position on the river crossing, blossomed in the early Middle Ages. By 1196, in the reign of Richard I, the bishop had gained permission to establish a weekly market here and had begun to develop the town to the north of the church on the grid of streets that can still be seen today. This left Holy Trinity itself in a slightly isolated position; but despite some competition in the fifteenth century from the Guild Chapel which, standing in the centre of town, was more convenient for the old and infirm, the church retained the loyalty of the increasingly prosperous townspeople, who continued to support it and contribute to its maintenance and enlargement.

And I have built
Two chantries, where sad and solemn priests
Sing still for Richard's soul.

(*HENRY V*, 4.1)

THE CHANTRY AND THE COLLEGE

John de Stratford was related to the powerful local Hatton family and, although he enjoyed a highly successful career within church and state – he was Archbishop of Canterbury from 1333 to 1348 and Chancellor of England in the 1330s – he appears, in common with many of his contemporaries, to have continued to hold his native town in great affection. In 1331, when he was Bishop of Winchester, he changed both the fortunes and the status of Stratford's parish church by founding and endowing a chantry chapel dedicated to St Thomas of Canterbury in its south aisle, which he rebuilt for the purpose, 'for the increase of Divine Service'.

Chantries were specifically established as foundations within which priests would say masses and pray for the souls of their benefactors. This practice had grown hugely after the rapid expansion in the early medieval period of monasteries which offered this lucrative service, and quickly developed beyond the monastic arm of the church. It became common for separate chantry foundations to be established either in private chapels or by taking over part of a larger church, and for a priest or groups of priests to be wholly devoted to this work. Kings and queens, great nobles and the rich would endow their chosen chantries, either during their lives or in the provisions they made in their wills, with often vast sums of money intended to ensure that masses were said for their souls in perpetuity – though those with smaller fortunes could make their

The college in an early nineteenth-century engraving.

The charnel house

There is now no trace, on the exterior north wall of the chancel, of the building that used to be attached to it there; and the opening in the north side of the chancel to the left of Shakespeare's memorial, which used to give access to it, is now blocked up, though the doorway itself and its elaborate, though desecrated, hoodmould survive.

The use to which this building was later put carries a particular resonance in view of the inscription on Shakespeare's gravestone (see pages 106ff), which sits only a few feet away from what was once its door inside the church. For the crypt of this building had become the charnel house, into which were piled the bones and skulls of earlier inhabitants of the graveyard which had to be displaced to make room for later burials.

Thomas Girtin, *The Ancient Charnel House, Stratford-upon-Avon.*

There is a painting of this building by Thomas Girtin (right); and Robert Bell Wheler, who published his *History and Antiquities of Stratford* in 1806, would have known it well. He describes it as 'a plain building 30ft long and 15ft wide, nearly the height of the chancel; and had every appearance of being the most ancient part of the church. This vault was built in the unornated Saxon Gothic style, the pillars a little above the surface of the earth were each divided into three ribs, intersecting each other, and closed up with unhewn stone. Above was a room supposed to be the bedroom appointed for the use of the four choristers; the ascent to which was by a flight of stone steps, and the general appearance of the building afforded some reason to believe that it was part of the church in being at the time of Edward the Confessor. In consequence of the dilapidated state of the building, a faculty was granted to raze it to the ground; and accordingly the bones were covered over and the charnel house taken down in the year 1800.'

It is unlikely that Wheler was right about the eleventh-century date, though it could certainly have predated the earliest surviving parts of the present building. But excavations on its site, reported in the *Stratford Herald* of December 10 1880, confirm its use: they revealed 'a roughly constructed arch... and when opened, human bones in a large crypt or charnel house'. Many of the bones were removed and reinterred in the churchyard, and the rest were covered over where they lay.

The connection between the inscription on Shakespeare's grave and the nearby charnel house was well known. The author of a book entitled *A tour through the island of Great Britain, interspersed with useful observations particularly fitted for the perusal of such as desire to travel over the island* wrote, 'I arrived in the month of July 1777 at the White Lion in Stratford supra Avon... At the side of the chancel is a charnel house almost filled with human bones, skulls etc... The guide said that Shakespeare was so affected by this charnel house that he wrote the epitaph for himself, to prevent his bones being thrown into it.'

If he did indeed write his own epitaph, it is certainly possible that it was intended to protect his remains from such a fate; and it is also possible, since his will merely specifies 'my body to the earth', that he had not prearranged a burial in the chancel for himself which, since burials inside churches were rarely disturbed, would have reassured him that it was unlikely to happen. In any event, his horror at the disinterment of bones from churchyards is evident in his plays. There is the scene in *Hamlet* when the sextons digging Ophelia's grave displace two skulls before coming across that of the court jester, Yorick; as Hamlet observes:

> That skull had a tongue in it and could sing once... and now my lady Worm's, chapless and knocked about the mazzard with a sexton's spade...
> Did these bones cost no more the breeding but to play at loggets with 'em. Mine ache to think on't.
>
> (*Hamlet*, 5.1)

And then there is Juliet:

> O, bid me leap, rather than marry Paris,
> From off the battlements of any tower...
> Or hide me nightly in a charnel house,
> O'ercovered quite with dead men's rattling bones,
> With reeky shanks and yellow chapless skulls.
>
> (*Romeo and Juliet*, 4.1)

Both warbling of one song, both in one key,
As if our hands, our sides, our voices, and minds
Had been incorporate.

(*A MIDSUMMER NIGHT'S DREAM*, 3.2)

endowments last for a fixed period, say for five or ten years after they died.

John de Stratford's initial foundation allowed for a warden, a sub-warden and three priests; five years later the number of priests was increased to eight, though it is not certain that this number was ever attained. John, along with other local worthies, endowed the chantry with lands, and purchased the patronage of the church for it from the Bishop of Worcester. Meanwhile a papal bull, issued in 1345, confirmed the chantry foundation and its link with the parish church.

In 1352 a house for the priests was built near the churchyard by John's nephew, Ralph de Stratford, Bishop of London 1340–54. This was the 'mansion place' seen by John Leland in about 1542, which he described as an 'ancient piece of work of square stone hard by the cemetery'. From this time the priests' house was known as the college and the church became The Collegiate Church of the Holy and Undivided Trinity, a title it still holds. The college building stood opposite the west end of the church, where the Methodist church and the parish hall now stand; and its name survives not only in the church's dedication but in the names of the streets round about.

The college of priests was enhanced under Ralph Collingwood, its dean from 1491 to 1518, by the appointment of 'four children choristers to be daily assistants in the celebration of divine service, which choristers should always come by two and two into the choir for Matins and Vespers… And for their better regulation he did order and appoint… that they should not be sent upon any occasion whatever into the town; that at dinner and supper they should be constantly in the college to wait at table; and to read upon the Bible or some other authentic book; that they should not come into the buttery to draw beer for themselves or anybody else; that after dinner they should go to the singing school; that their master should be one of the priests or clerks appointed by the discretion of the warden, being a man able to instruct them in singing to the organ.'

Collingwood donated land for the maintenance of the choristers and appointed trustees to look after their welfare. He also ordained that 'they should have one bedchamber in the church whereunto they were to repair in winter-time at eight of the clock, and in summer at nine; in which lodging to be two beds, wherein they were to sleep by couples; and that before they did put off their clothes they should all say the prayer of *De profundis* with a loud voice, with the prayers and orisons of the faithful, and afterwards say thus "God have mercy on the soul of Ralph Collingwood, our founder, and Master Thomas Balshall, a special benefactor to the same".'

This bedchamber was the room on the first floor of the old building attached to the north side of the chancel which Shakespeare almost certainly knew as a charnel house (see box opposite). After the choristers left, the room became the minister's study, before the whole building was adjudged to be too rickety and it was demolished.

Chantries were among the assets of the church that Henry VIII coveted when he needed to raise money for his wars, and they were included in the survey of 1534–5 designed to establish the church's worth. At that time the Stratford college was valued at £128 9s 1d, and was staffed by a dean, a sub-warden, three chaplains, three clerks and four choristers. Chantries were finally abolished by an Act passed in 1545, at the end of Henry's reign; but it was left to his successor, Edward VI, to finalise their dissolution in 1547. The Holy Trinity college and chantry were then valued at £123 11s 9d.

The holder of the Holy Trinity living now became a 'vicar' rather than a warden or dean. The college building itself was granted by Elizabeth I to Richard Coninsby, and at the end of his lease it was sold to John Combe, who lived in it till his death in 1614. This was the John Combe who is buried in the chancel and was a money-lender and a friend of Shakespeare. After his death the building stayed with the Combe family until one of them married a Clopton and it passed into that family. It then went through various hands until it was demolished in 1799.

Between two funerals

Thomas Balsall, who was dean of the college and vicar of the church, served at Holy Trinity from 1466 until his death in 1491. It was he who gave the church much of its present form: he rebuilt the chancel and the porch, and laid the foundations for the work on the nave and clerestory carried out by his successor, Ralph Collingwood. He lies now in the splendid tomb he built for himself in the chancel, to the left of the altar.

Pre-Reformation glass in the north-east chancel window.

William Shakespeare died just over a century after Balsall, and is buried only a few feet away from him, in his grave in the chancel. But the appearance of the church and the forms of worship that Balsall knew had already, by the time of Shakespeare's burial, broadly disappeared. Within a mere 100 years or so, churchgoing had changed.

When you came into the church on a Sunday in Balsall's time, 500 or so years ago, you found a real feast for the senses. Firstly touch: entering through the porch you dipped your hand into a large bowl of holy water, touching it to your forehead and making the sign of the cross. The remains of the holy water stoups are still there to this day. Your fingers reached for your prayer beads, the rosary, and then hearing took over: your ears heard the organ playing and the plainsong chanting of the priests in the choir or chancel, their part of the church beyond the great rood screen. But the language you heard was not the language of everyday: all the words of the chants and the mass were in Latin, which only the educated among the congregation knew.

Then eyes: you were looking at the biggest space for miles around, part of the biggest building you knew. The nave – unencumbered by chairs and pews – was the people's church, used as a meeting place for the town as well as for services: 'A natural place for meeting your friends, a supernatural place for meeting with God' (Owen Chadwick). The pillars were alive with multi-coloured designs, and the walls and windows were decorated with pictures of the saints and scenes from the Bible. All the altars of the church were dressed in their own hangings, lit by flickering candles and tapers, and great colourful banners hung around the church and were carried in processions. Candles lit the statues and pictures of saints, and higher than them all, in the great archway at the head of the nave, stood the rood – the figure of Christ on the cross, with Mary and John to either side.

Your sense of smell was well and truly engaged as the service started, as clouds of incense spread through the church, lingering in the nose and floating above the heads of the celebrants and the congregation. The Eucharistic Prayer was the liturgical highpoint when all senses were awoken together. Bells rang in the chancel and from the bell chamber in the tower as the priest elevated the host, the body of Christ. People craned to see this holy sight, as God came among them in the form of bread and wine; but it was not easy to see, as the celebrant was far away through the rood screen at the high altar in the chancel.

Only the priest, however, was to taste the body and blood of Christ; the people received the bread only on Easter Day and on their deathbed. Now their sense of taste had to be satisfied with the kiss of peace, as they came forward to kiss the Pax Brede, a silver disc with Christ's image on it, and in the sharing of a loaf at the end of the service, baked at home by a different parish family each week and blessed by the priest at the altar. It was the first food many of them had eaten that day.

How things had changed when Shakespeare was buried here. Salvation now came through hearing and digesting the word of God, which at least was now proclaimed in English. All the ornament and the colour were gone – the banners, the images of the saints, the holy water, the sculptures, the organs, the candles, the vestments, the incense, the great crucifix; all had been removed or defaced. The walls were white, the pillars grey. The beautiful carvings on Balsall's tomb showing scenes from the life of Christ were smashed and broken. The aim now was to block out all distractions and encourage the worshippers to focus on the pulpit and the preacher. 'Let sense be dumb, let flesh retire' is a phrase from a more recent hymn, but expresses well that distrust of the body and its sensuality that seemed to be writ large in much of the destruction within churches at that time.

God's word is, of course, the path to salvation, but the changes wrought by those sixteenth-century reformers seemed to indicate that there were no other ways through which God could reach us. Much undoubtedly needed reforming, but faith had begun to seem accessible only to those who could listen and concentrate, read and understand; for those who could not worship in that way, religion had somehow got much harder and bleaker. Something of the mystery and awe, as well as the sheer sensuality, of medieval worship was lost at that turbulent time.

Now, 400 years later, a lot has changed again, as the Church of England has regained its inheritance as a church both Catholic and Reformed. Neither Balsall nor Shakespeare would recognise all that today's worshippers in Holy Trinity find so familiar, although equally there is much that they would still know. It is a testament to the weight of history that this church carries that we today can still somehow imagine what it was like to be present at those two funerals, separated by a mere 125 years, and how differently we would have experienced them.

Martin Gorick: Extract from sermon series 'Between two funerals', 2006

Above: The Clopton Chapel.

Left: Thomas Balsall's tomb.

You still shall live – such virtue hath my pen –
Where breath most breathes, even in the
mouths of men.

(SONNET 81)

SHAKESPEARE AND TOURISM

Holy Trinity church was now once again, post-Reformation, simply the parish church of Stratford, although it kept the 'Collegiate' appellation. But within only a few decades, the burial in its chancel of a towering literary figure, whose fame rapidly grew during the years after his death, gave it an added dimension and a following not usually to be found in 'ordinary' parish churches. While it remained – and remains to this day – the place where the majority of Stratford's Anglicans worshipped, and worship, its clergy and custodians found themselves having to cope with a growing tide of visitors to William Shakespeare's grave and monument.

New Place

This was the 'pretty house of brick and timber' which Hugh Clopton built for himself in 1483. With its five gables, it was the second largest house in Stratford. Shakespeare bought it in 1597 for an estimated £120, and it was where he died in 1616.

It was left to his daughter, Susanna Hall, and then passed to her daughter, Elizabeth, whose husband, Thomas Nash, owned the house next door. It came back into the Clopton family when Sir John Clopton inherited it in 1676 through his wife, Barbara Walker, daughter of its then owner Sir Edward Walker, Garter King of Arms. John Clopton rebuilt it for his son, Hugh, and is on record as having been happy to open it up to Shakespeare tourists.

However, it then fell into the hands of the Reverend Francis Gastrell, the retired vicar of Frodsham, who became so enraged at the constant stream of tourists that in 1759 he cut down the mulberry tree in the garden that was said to have been planted by Shakespeare. The furious people of Stratford retaliated by smashing his windows. But worse was to follow when he fell into dispute with the Corporation about the rates they wished to charge him for the house. He razed New Place to the ground, and it is said that he found himself forced to leave the town.

That these were becoming what is now known as a 'visitor attraction' was recognised within a few years of the poet's death. The first 'touristy' mention of the monument dates to 1634, when one Lieutenant Hammond wrote in his journal of seeing the 'neat monument' in the church while he was in Stratford as part of a lengthy countrywide tour. In the 1660s the vicar of Holy Trinity, John Ward, decided to make a point of reading the plays and keeping notebooks with references to Shakespeare, presumably as a response to growing numbers of visitors to Stratford and the grave in the church: 'Remember to peruse Shakespeare's plays, and be versed in them that I may not be ignorant in the matter.'

John Ward aside, other incumbents may perhaps be seen as tolerating the Shakespeare pilgrims rather than encouraging them. But Garrick's Shakespeare Jubilee of 1769, which became famous across Europe and the USA and well as within Britain, coincided with the awakening interest of Holy Trinity vicars in the poet and really marked the beginning of the Shakespeare legend in Stratford. And when James Davenport became vicar shortly after that event, in 1787, he began to show real interest in the connection between the church and the poet. Davenport, who was to serve at Stratford for fifty-four years, worked hard to raise popular awareness of Shakespeare and his grave in Holy Trinity. Writing to Edmond Malone, the Shakespearian editor who had just brought out an edition of the plays, he said, 'You do me justice in supposing I should be ready to give you every information in my power concerning our immortal bard and his connections.' He was true to his word, and maintained a lengthy correspondence with Malone about Shakespeare, as well as encouraging others to recognise the importance of Holy Trinity in what was rapidly becoming a flourishing tourist industry centred on Shakespeare's connections with Stratford.

The church was, in fact, the main focus of Shakespeare pilgrims at this time. Although the birthplace in Henley Street, and Shakespeare's own house, New Place, were (while the latter existed – see box) recognised by both townspeople and visitors as important relics of the poet, the church was

View of the sanctuary from the priest's door, *c* 1850. Colour lithograph by Leighton Brothers.

usually the first port of call. One William Hall, who arrived one evening in 1694, made it his priority on the next day 'to visit the ashes of the great Shakespeare which lie interred in that church'. He wrote about his visit in a letter to a friend, and added that 'they have laid him full seventeen-foot deep, deep enough to secure him'.

This preference for the church was partly because, as a public building, it was much more easily accessible than what were still then private houses; but the poet's grave was also, according to the tenor of the times, much more desirable as a shrine, not only because it held the mortal remains of the great one, but because it could also give rise to earnest contemplations of the fleeting nature of life and the triumph of Art over Death.

Davenport's interest in Shakespeare, and his willingness to help researchers and enquirers, lasted all his life, and he was also the first to encourage celebrations of the poet's birthday. The value of the connection was evident towards the end of his incumbency in the 1830s, when the fabric of the building and the state of the monument and the grave had become a cause for concern, and he was able to use Shakespeare's name to raise funds both locally and in London for the urgent work that was needed. The successful response in the capital to that appeal made it clear that Holy Trinity was a major player in the Shakespeare industry in Stratford.

The extraordinary Delia Bacon episode in 1856 (see page 125) demonstrates that interest in Shakespeare and his life and death in Stratford was no longer just a British matter but had spread worldwide. And the church came even more into its own when the mid-Victorian fascination with the poet's home town found its culmination in 1864 with the

Other Shakespeare 'visitor attractions' in Stratford

Shakespeare's birthplace and family home in Henley Street was purchased in 1847 by what is now The Shakespeare Birthplace Trust, and the other four local houses with connections to the poet – Nash's House, with the New Place gardens (purchased in 1862), Anne Hathaway's Cottage (1892), Hall's Croft (1950) and Mary Arden's House (1968) – are also now part of The Shakespeare Birthplace Trust's charitable remit for perpetual guardianship. Shakespeare's schoolroom in the Guildhall, now part of King Edward VI Grammar School where the education of boys has gone on uninterrupted for over 450 years, is also now sometimes open to visitors.

John Keats

John Keats visited Stratford on October 2 1817 while staying in Oxford with his friend Benjamin Bailey. Although the record of his visit to Shakespeare's Birthplace survived in its visitors' book, where he gave his address as 'everywhere', it had been assumed that the record of his visit to Holy Trinity church had been lost. But in fact it has been languishing relatively undisturbed in the archives of The Shakespeare Birthplace Trust, where it has once again come to light – and it reveals that, in the context of Shakespeare's grave and the church where he worshipped, Keats chose to use the Latin '*ubique*' rather than the English 'everywhere' for his enigmatic address. This choice of Latin might suggest that Keats regarded Shakespeare not just as his muse but as a presiding saint. Earlier that same year, on May 11, Keats had concluded a letter to his friend Benjamin Haydon with: 'So now in the Name of Shakespeare Raphael and all our Saints I commend you to the care of heaven!'

Paul Edmondson

Visitors' books for, right, Shakespeare's Birthplace and, above right, Holy Trinity.

celebrations for the tercentenary of his birth. The Holy Trinity vicar at the time, George Granville, was at the centre of the planning for this event, and for the first time the church played a religious part, with two special services and sermons on the theme of Shakespeare and God by the Archbishop of Dublin and the Bishop of St Andrews; the collections raised over £60 for the repair of the chancel.

The Shakespeare industry was now in full swing. However, there was to be ongoing controversy when the vicar who took office in 1867, John Day Collis, instituted admission charges.

Visitors had previously been guided round the church and the monuments by the parish clerk and other helpers, who expected some remuneration for their services; indeed, they appear to have profited so much from the work that they were referred to as 'money-changers'. Collis took over this source of income, and in 1871/2 paid for new gas fittings for the chancel 'out of the balance of the visitors' fees for last year and this'. But then in 1877 he took the more radical step of charging 6d – a considerable sum of money then – for admission to the chancel itself. This caused universal outrage, with thunderings in the press. Although parishioners were never charged a fee, the local *Stratford Herald* declared that the vicar 'in turning his church into a common show-place… is a scandal to the town. It savours so much of Barnum' (the nineteenth-century American showman and circus-owner).

But Collis could see that admission charges would be of great help in funding the desperately needed repair and improvement of the church, the cost of which in 1877 was estimated at £15,000. Among the work the charges helped to pay for at this time was the replacement of the altar rails and their repositioning 'so as to afford protection to the slab covering Shakespeare's tomb'.

Remuneration – O, that's the Latin for three-farthings.

(*LOVE'S LABOUR'S LOST*, 3.1)

Collis's successor in 1879, George Arbuthnot, saw no reason to retreat from the decision to charge 'the great number of strangers who come, not to pray, but to see the grave of our great poet', though 'we must not forget that the building is the Church of Almighty God, and not a mere monument erected to the fame of a man, however illustrious'. Although opponents of the charge contended that Holy Trinity 'is no ordinary parish church… it may be said to belong to the whole of the civilised world', Arbuthnot was quite happy to balance its fame as a literary shrine with its function as a local parish church, and to use that fame as a means of fundraising. His successor, William Gardner Melville, continued to deny free access to the grave by having a cord placed across the end of the choir stalls after Sunday service, in order to deny admission to those who, he perceived, had attended the service only in order to gain access to the chancel and the grave afterwards. But Tom Noel Prentice, Melville's successor, obviously felt more than a bit uncomfortable about the charge, and was inclined to hedge it about with attempts at justification. During his incumbency there was a notice on the door which read 'This church is open daily for worship and meditation' and 'the custodian is authorised to admit without charge'. In the parish magazine he pointed out that, although the notice on the church door asked those who came to see the grave to pay 6d each towards upkeep, 'the words are "asked to" not "must"… there is no charge, but my word, isn't that 6d useful?' The issue could still clearly raise hackles, and under Tom Bland, Prentice's successor, there was a complete reversal of policy. Revenue collection was left to the generosity of visitors. This at first seemed to work, as receipts increased and the vicar reported 'a very much nicer atmosphere as visitors enter the church'; but by 1968, when faced with a repair bill of £100,000, Bland had to accept that the charge must be reimposed. Visitors still pay it; and some of them still object!

There's place and means for every man alive.

(*ALL'S WELL THAT ENDS WELL*, 4.3)

The church, over the centuries since Shakespeare was buried there, has become an inextricable part of the tourist industry centred on him – though visitors are also encouraged to spend time in the church itself, and to recognise that it is a fine medieval building, with splendid architecture and artefacts and much to say about the history of religion in England. The evidence of the leaflets about the church which are dispensed to visitors at the donation point, when they are invited to make a donation to see the chancel, the grave and the monument, is indicative of the worldwide reach that Holy Trinity now has: the leaflets have been translated so far into twenty-five languages, including Chinese and Japanese as well as all the major European and east European languages. Holy Trinity is indeed 'a parish for the world'.

An illustration from the late nineteenth century which shows the Shakespeare family gravestones and the old altar rail.

THE CLOPTON

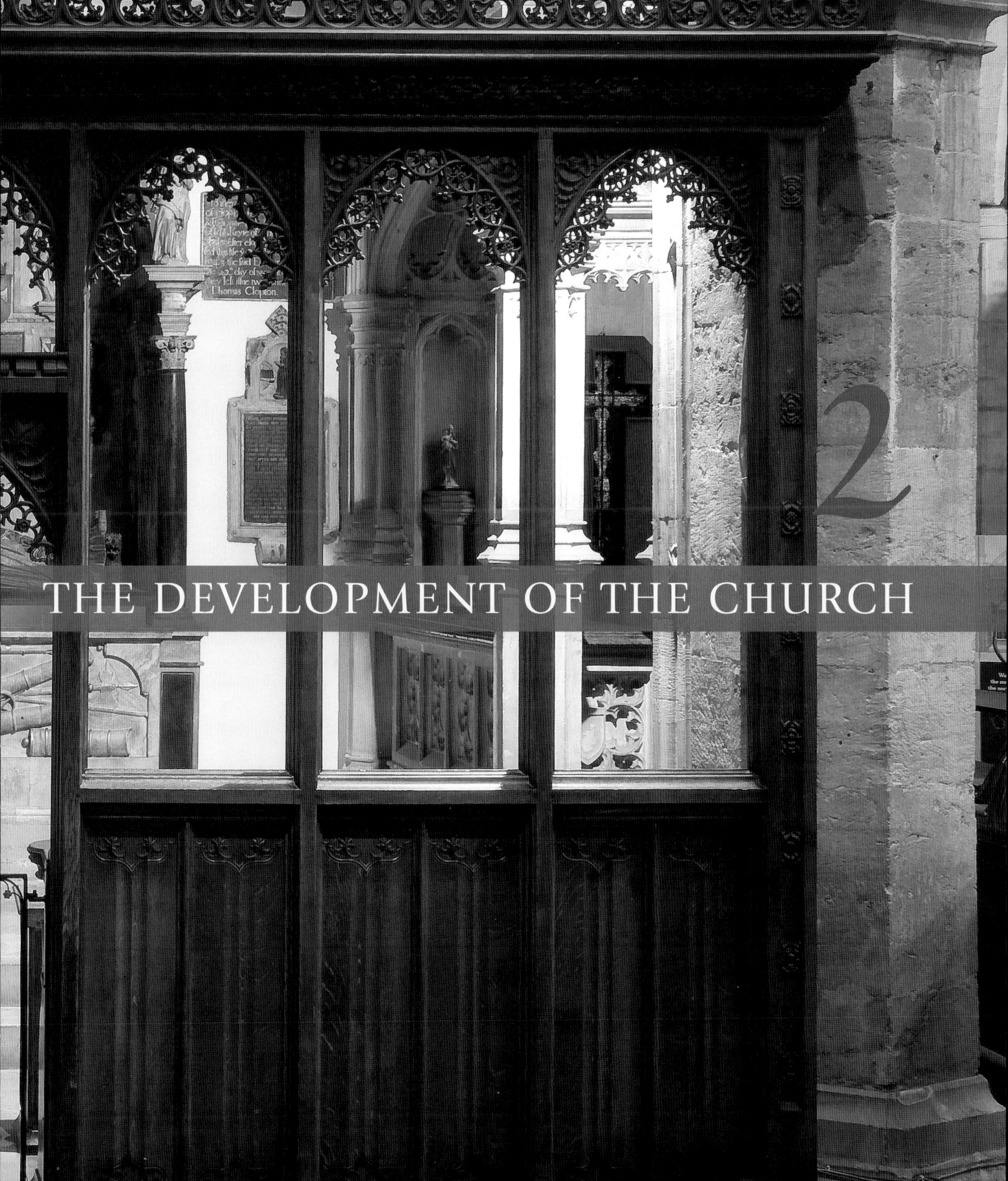

2

THE DEVELOPMENT OF THE CHURCH

Tongues in trees, books in the running brooks,
Sermons in stones, and good in everything.

(AS YOU LIKE IT, 2.1)

Holy Trinity church enjoys an idyllic setting, a little away from the bustle of Stratford town centre and right on the bank of the Avon, with its swans and ducks, its willows, the water meadows on the opposite bank and its visitors messing around in boats. The gardens next to it, the property of the Royal Shakespeare Company, have a brass rubbing centre and green open spaces where open-air plays are performed or people simply enjoy lounging in the sunshine.

There are three gates into the churchyard, one each on the north, west and south sides. The one used by most visitors is opposite the Parish Centre in Old Town and leads through an avenue of limes to the north porch. Ancient graves sit on either side, and there are vaults underfoot beneath the slabs that form the path, some of which are inscribed with the names of those buried below. The limes themselves represent, on the left, the twelve tribes of Israel and, on the right, the twelve Apostles; as is traditional with this iconography, one of

Top left: The stone pine from Ravenna.

Left: River Avon from the church.

Opposite: The east facade.

The path to the north porch, flanked by the lime avenue.

the limes on the right is set back, representing both Judas leaving the ranks of the Apostles and Matthias joining them. The current avenue was replanted in 1993/4.

The other main gate opens further down Old Town into a path which leads to the west door. This path was improved in 1887 and named Jubilee Way in honour of Queen Victoria's golden jubilee; the lime trees which still line it were planted by John Day Collis, vicar 1867–79. There are two other spectacular trees here, both planted about a century ago by one of the curates: the one by the west door is a cedar from Gethsemane, while a little further round towards the south facade of the church is a stone pine from Ravenna that has grown into a curiously convoluted shape.

Visitors can walk all round the church, sit and watch the world go by on the bank of the river and enjoy the ancient lichen-encrusted gravestones and the shady trees and shrubs. Regular burials in the churchyard ceased at the end of the nineteenth century, though there have been some recent exceptions when a fortuitous discovery of a couple of hitherto forgotten plots accommodated the burial of Dennis Spiller, who had died while still incumbent in 1992, and shortly afterwards that of Vernon Nicholls, retired bishop of Sodor and Man, and his wife. The atmosphere is one of peace and tranquillity – enhanced, perhaps, by the frisson of knowing that under one's feet lie the remains of Hamnet Shakespeare and Judith Quiney, as well as the poet's mother and father, sister and brothers, and many others who would have known William Shakespeare merely as their neighbour in Stratford, not as the iconic poet and playwright honoured worldwide today.

Puck: Now it is the time of night
That the graves, all gaping wide,
Every one lets forth his sprite
In the churchway paths to glide.

(*A MIDSUMMER NIGHT'S DREAM*, 5.2)

THE BUILDING

The tower, the crossing and the transepts

Although the first written records of the present church date to 1332, when John de Stratford rebuilt the south aisle, it is known that the transepts and crossing were built over a century earlier, around 1210. The lancet windows in both north and south transepts are early thirteenth-century in date, and the remains of two arches of the same date can be seen in the inner corners of the north transept, abutting the piers supporting the tower. The tower was probably rebuilt at this time too. Harvey Bloom, the vicar of Whitchurch who in 1902 published *Shakespeare's Church*, the only previous history of the church, tells us that the work was done in a piecemeal fashion as money became available; he records that funds for all the building work at this time, and later when the aisles were being rebuilt, were raised by various supportive bishops granting indulgences – remission of time in Purgatory – to all who contributed to the costs.

A relic of the older church within the north transept.

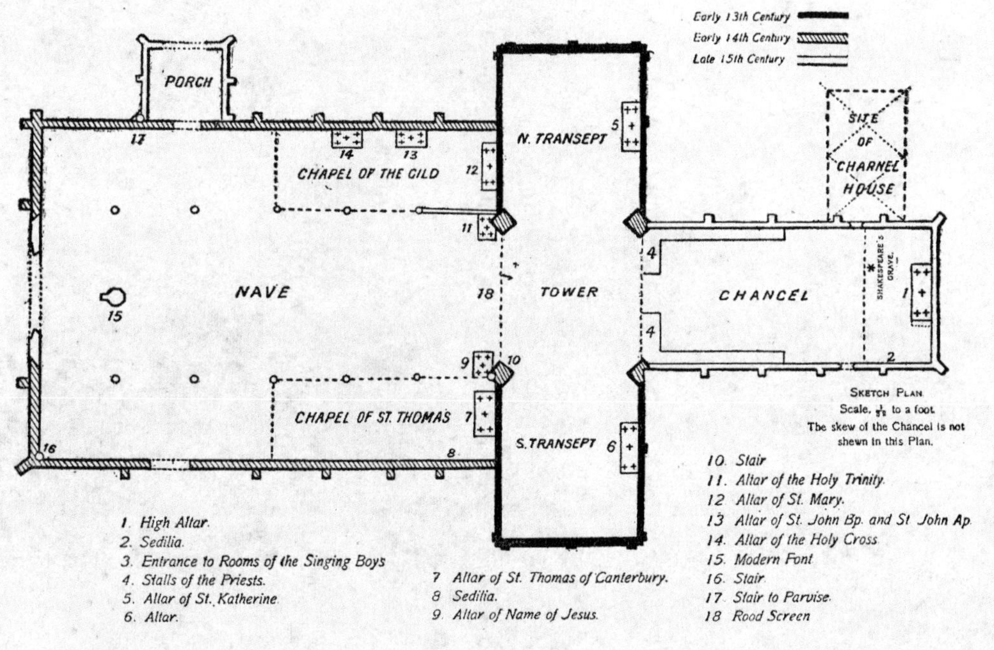

Plan of the church, in Harvey Bloom's 1902 history, *Shakespeare's Church.*

Above: The rood screen; below, one of the ancient masks that probably adorned the chancel ceiling.
Opposite: The chancel seen from the nave.

The upper storey of the tower, with its circular windows each filled with a different design in plate tracery – where stone rather than glass is the dominant feature – was added about 100 years later. Engravings show that the original steeple was a somewhat stumpy affair made of wood covered with lead; at only forty-two feet high, it was out of proportion with the rest of the church, so it was replaced in Warwick hewn stone in 1763.

The north transept is now used as a choir vestry, sealed off from the church by the original rood screen, which once separated the crossing from the nave and was moved to its current position in 1842. This screen, which is of excellent fourteenth-century craftsmanship, was originally surmounted by the rood loft and the rood cross, and its solidity reminds us of what would once have been the layout of the church: up to the rood was the people's domain, where mass was heard, parishioners met and interacted, the church court held its sessions and general parish business went on; beyond the rood, sealed off and private, was the priests' world where offices were sung and private masses said. The two ancient masks which hang on the screen probably came from the original chancel roof, which Wheler records as having been 'profusely ornamented with curious figures'; and the screen now between the crossing and the chancel is another ancient survival and a good example of late fifteenth-century work.

The Harbert memorial in the north transept.

An aumbry and a piscina are still to be found on the east wall of the north transept; and it also houses a remarkable monument to Thomas Harbert and his wife Elizabeth. The inscription reads:

> On the North Side of this wall
> lye the Bodys of THOMAS HARBERT Carver
> and ELIZABETH his Wife
> She died June the 3d 1736 Aged 76
> He died June the 6th 1738 Aged near 80

So far, so ordinary. But above the inscription, surrounding an escutcheon, is what appears at first sight to be a sunburst, except that closer inspection reveals that the rays of the sun are actually a carver's tools – all manner of chisels, saws, measuring tools, hammers and so on: a fitting memorial to a man who seems to have been a craftsman of a high order.

The crossing is octagonal in form, as are the two fonts now in the church, representing the six days of creation and a day of rest (the Sabbath), with the eighth side standing for the new creation heralded by the Resurrection. The small door in the south-west pillar leads up to the ringing chamber, and some faint remnants of medieval wall paintings can be seen on the pillar to its left. Some of the steps up to the bell chamber still have traces of carving on their undersides, which indicates that they are probably reused pieces of earlier church fabric.

In the corners and at the top of the arches in the crossing ceiling can be seen several 'green men', now picked out in gilding. These are faces which have leaves instead of hair and often more leaves coming out of their mouths. They are rather obviously pre-Christian in origin, but their frequent appearance in churches and cathedrals all over the country indicates that they were adopted by the medieval church to symbolise incarnation, resurrection and renewal.

The fine brass candelabrum which hangs from the centre of the crossing ceiling was the gift, in 1720, of 'Mrs Sarah Woolmer wife of Joseph Woolmer of this Corporation'; the dedication is engraved on the ball at its base, and its twenty or so branches are surmounted by an eagle. The name Woolmer can be seen in many memorials in the church, and one Joseph Woolmer was buried in the chancel, according to the 1836 plan of the graves there (see page 81). As the plan does not date the gravestone it is not clear whether that Joseph Woolmer was Sarah's husband, although her husband was almost certainly one of several Woolmers who donated valuable communion plate in 1716, four years before his wife's gift.

Right: The candelabrum. Above it can be seen the Three Fish symbol of the Holy Trinity, by Jim Dawes, woodcarver and church member.

Below: The door to the ringing chamber.

Below centre: Remnants of pre-Reformation wall painting in the crossing.

Below right: The underside of one of the stairs leading up to the ringing chamber.

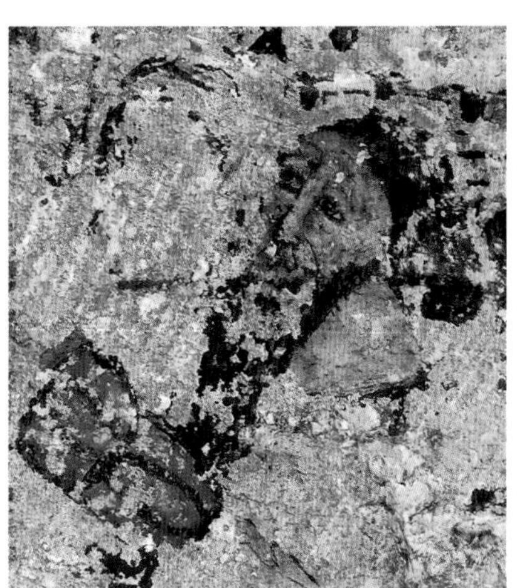

Left: An Arts and Crafts aumbry in the vestry in the south transept.

Below: Part of the American window in the south transept.

Part of the south transept has been closed off to form the clergy vestry, and the rest of it is now dedicated to St Peter and set aside for private worship and weekday morning prayers. The screen to the transept forms part of the First World War memorial designed by the church architect Guy Pemberton.

The stained glass window in the south transept, installed in 1896, is known as the American window since it was paid for by gifts from Americans. It portrays the Madonna and Child and the Adoration of the Magi at its centre, with English and American holy men occupying the outer lights, including Archbishop Laud, who was the first to suggest sending a bishop to America, plus Amerigo Vespucci, Christopher Columbus, William Penn and the Pilgrim Fathers landing at Plymouth Rock. Also depicted are St Eric, Bishop of Greenland, and Dr Samuel Seabury, first Bishop of Connecticut. Underneath is inscribed 'The Gentiles shall come to thy light, and the Kings to thy brightness. AMDG The Gift of America to Shakespeare's Church'.

These our actors,
As I foretold you, were all spirits, and
Are melted into air, into thin air.

(*THE TEMPEST*, 4.1)

Two memorials in the south transept, separated in date by over 300 years, are worthy of note. The earlier one is the epitaph of Richard Hill, a bailiff and draper, who died in 1593 (the year that Shakespeare's name first burst into print with the publication of his narrative poem *Venus and Adonis*). It sits on the wall in a shallow alcove, and the lettering is in some places worn away to illegibility. The inscription starts with a text from Job in Hebrew:

> And naked shall I return thither: the Lord gave, and the Lord hath taken away; blessed be the name of the Lord

Quatrains in Greek and Latin follow, and then comes a longer text in English. The multilingual nature of the dedication argues for a high level of education in both dedicator and dedicatee, despite the inaccuracy of some of the Greek. The English reads as follows:

> Heare borne heare lived heare died and buried heare
> Liethe Richarde Hil thrise bailif of this borrow
> Too matrones of good fame he married in Gode's feare
> And now releast in joi he reasts from worldlie sorrow
> Heare lieth intombd the corps of Richarde Hill
> A woollen draper being in his time
> Whose virtues live whose fame dooth florish stil
> Though hee desolved be to dust and slime
> A mirror he and paterne mai be made
> For such as shall suckcead him in that trade
> He did not use to sweare to glose eather faigne
> His brother to defraude in barganinge
> Hee woold not strive to get excessive gaine
> In ani cloath or other kinde of thinge
> His servant I this trueth can testifie
> A witness that beheld it with mi eie

The other is a plaque 'In grateful memory of the players who fell in the Great War 1914–1919', engraved with a poem by Rudyard Kipling; it was unveiled in 1925.

> We counterfeited once for your disport
> Mens' joy and sorrow; but our day has passed
> We pray you pardon all where we fell short
> Seeing we were your servants to this last

Above: Part of the Hebrew and Greek inscriptions on the Hill memorial.
Below: The Kipling poem.

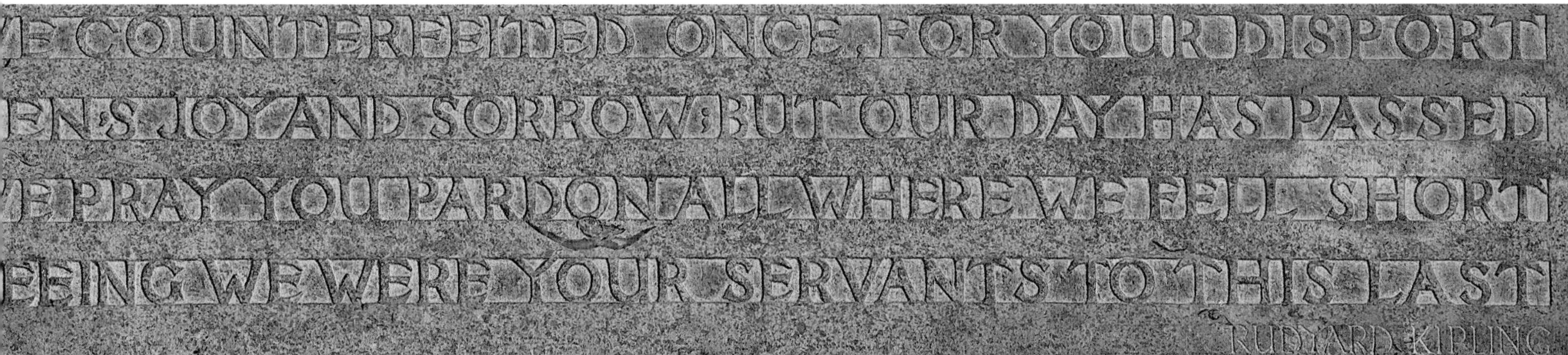

The nave and clerestories

The arcades of the nave, like the aisles, date to the early fourteenth century. The clerestories to north and south above them are late fifteenth-century in date, the work of Ralph Collingwood, who became dean in 1491 and carried on the rebuilding of the church which had been instigated by his predecessor, Thomas Balsall. He is also credited with rebuilding the west wall.

The high, light clerestories are typically Perpendicular in style, with their stone shafts elegantly rising from carved angels at the intersection of the nave arches to the corbels that support the roof. The elongated angels themselves show their Perpendicular origin, as does the stone tracery adorning the panels under the windows. The Perpendicular style can also be seen on the exterior of the fine original oak west doors. Both south and north clerestories have been restored within the last hundred years, with the work involving the careful

Above and opposite: The Perpendicular architecture of the nave.

Left: Original late fifteenth-century glass in the north clerestory.

Opposite: The west window.
Below: The west facade.
Below right: The pulpit.

Be stone no more. Approach.
Strike all that look upon with marvel
(*THE WINTER'S TALE*, 5.3)

The green marble pulpit standing at the south-eastern corner of the nave was the gift of Sir Theodore Martin in honour of his wife, the celebrated Shakespearian actress Helen Faucit, who died in 1898. In August 1899, in a letter to the mayor, Sir Arthur Hodgson, he offered the large sum of £1000 for a new pulpit, with the stipulation that he should be consulted about its design and positioning. The gift was very welcome, but it took some time for the details to be sorted out, and it was not until March 1900 that the

repair and replacement of the stone tracery where necessary. When the north clerestory was restored in 2009, the glass was all painstakingly removed, cleaned and reset in new leaded lights. The vicar was delighted to learn from Nick Beacham, the master glazier, that almost all of the glass was original, dating from the 1490s when the clerestories were built.

The three niches set above the exterior of the west door into the tracery of the west window are an unusual feature. The stained glass in this window was installed in the late nineteenth century, when George Arbuthnot was vicar. It depicts the twelve apostles surrounding the central figure of Christ being baptised by John the Baptist. Over his head hovers the dove, the representation of the Holy Spirit, and to the left is an angelic figure, there to represent the voice of God the Father saying 'This is my beloved son, in whom I am well pleased'. The window is therefore doubly significant: firstly depicting baptism while overlooking the font and the baptismal area of the church; and secondly portraying the Holy Trinity to whom the church is dedicated.

Faucit memorial controversies

Sir Theodore Martin's pulpit was not universally liked. The vicar, George Arbuthnot, refused to attend the dedication service since he did not approve of the design and would have preferred it to have been made of carved oak. As late as November 1907, on the news of the death of its designer, George Bodley, Arbuthnot still expressed regret that 'he had allowed himself to permit the pulpit to be introduced'.

As soon as it was consecrated, it was announced that Sir Theodore had been granted permission to erect a second memorial to his wife, an effigy to be placed opposite the bust of Shakespeare in the chancel. He had promised £500 to the church restoration fund on condition that his wife's memorial there should face that of Shakespeare, and the Bishop of Worcester had agreed – though it was apparently 'to his shame'. Once again the vicar disapproved, though the bishop overruled him; but there was also an upsurge of local opposition, not least from the novelist Marie Corelli, who wrote to the local press in outrage at the proposal. In November Sir Theodore withdrew his offer in view of 'the unseemly controversy which has arisen'. The memorial itself can still be seen in the Royal Shakespeare Theatre.

In May 1901 there was more bad feeling, this time because the figure of St Jerome on the pulpit had been 'mutilated'. He had been furnished with a crozier, although he was not a bishop, and the vicar had insisted that the top of his staff should be filed off in the cause of ecclesiastical accuracy. This had been done in April, and provoked a storm of letters in the local press; but it was not until October that Sir Theodore was informed about what had happened and wrote to complain.

In his history of the church, Bloom is scathing about the pulpit, which he regarded as 'not such as the canons of good taste would have selected, which is the more to be deplored since the offering was a costly one and a memorial to a distinguished lady'. He was particularly rude about the ecclesiology used in the depiction of the saints: 'St Jerome... retains the absurdity of a cardinal's hat with one set of hauppes, and those tied beneath the chin, instead of depending on either side'; and St Helena is apparently holding too many Passion nails: three, when 'one is frequent'.

St Jerome.

St Helena.

work was commissioned; the designer was George Bodley, of Bodley and Garner, who had been the consulting architect on the works to the church since the mid-1880s. The central alabaster statue of the five on the facade is of St Helena, mother of the Emperor Constantine and finder of the true cross, but the face is Helen Faucit's. Faucit herself was particularly well known for playing Hermione in *The Winter's Tale*, and wrote movingly about posing as Hermione's statue, which comes to life in the final scene. Here on the pulpit the famous actress is cast as another statue, and is centrally placed where the word of God is brought to life by the preacher.

The aisles

Both north and south aisles began to take their present form in the early fourteenth century when John de Stratford widened them and established his chantry chapel in the south aisle.

The east end of the north aisle originally held a chapel with three altars dedicated to the Holy Cross, the Blessed Virgin Mary and, jointly, to St John the Baptist and St John the Apostle. This was where the priests attached to the town guilds, in particular the Guild of the Holy Cross, said mass. The north aisle was the first to be reconstructed, between 1312 and 1316, and was probably the expression in Stratford of the growing cult of the Virgin Mary, which was resulting at the time in the building of grand Lady Chapels in churches and cathedrals all over the country. The suppression of this cult at the Reformation, along with the dissolution of the guilds, caused the altars to be removed and the rich furnishings that adorned the chapels to be confiscated. Hugh Clopton had already, in the 1490s, built his own tomb there, under the nave arch at the east end of the aisle, and that area now became the memorial chapel for the Clopton family.

The Lady Chapel

In Thomas Balsall's time, the north aisle held an altar dedicated to the Blessed Virgin Mary, the mother of Jesus. We know there was a large statue of Mary there, and that candles burnt there day and night, a real focus of devotion for the people of the town. At the Reformation all this was swept away. Devotion involving saints and images became suspect, and they were taken away and destroyed as idolatrous. It seems strange to us today, but in the name of God it was decreed that every image of Jesus and his mother should be thrown out of this church, or left mutilated and defaced.

The Lady Altar is still there; but you can hardly see it. On its surface are huge statues of King James I's Master of the Ordnance and his wife, whose bodies are now buried beneath it. On the front of the altar you can see cannonballs, pikes and muskets, the tools of his trade. The statue of Mary, a feminine symbol of holiness, humility and hospitality, was thrown out as idolatrous – and ironically, in her place, we now have even bigger graven images, this time distinctly masculine symbols of wealth, power and military strength.

The powerful religious forces that swept through Holy Trinity 450 years ago have muted through time; dogma and patterns of worship have changed, and no one now, at least within the Christian west, would take a chisel to a 'graven image' (though it still happens elsewhere…). And now we have a new statue of Mary in what was our Lady Chapel – small, to be sure, and standing at the side of the chapel rather than in the prominent central position she once occupied. But she reminds us of what was once there, and of how our forefathers in this church venerated and honoured her.

Martin Gorick: Extract from sermon series 'Between two funerals', 2006

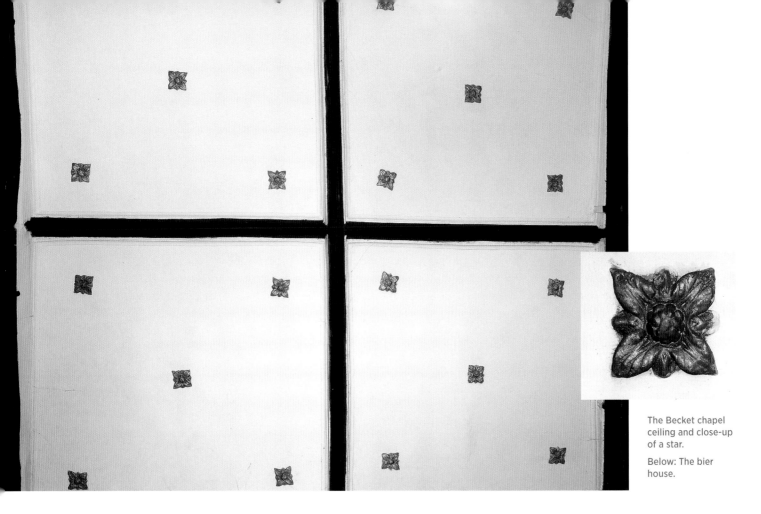

The Becket chapel ceiling and close-up of a star.

Below: The bier house.

The south aisle now retains little of the splendour it would once have displayed when it was the home of the chantry chapel founded by John de Stratford and dedicated to St Thomas of Canterbury. The Becket Chapel stood against the east wall of the aisle, with its original western extent marked by the stars on the ceiling. The original form of the aisle was obliterated when the organ was moved to this position at the end of the nineteenth century – though the roof here is the oldest in the church, dating to the early fourteenth century when the aisle was rebuilt.

The sedilia on the south wall are Victorian replicas; when the scaffolding erected to carry out repairs on the clerestory windows was being taken down in 1940, the date 1840 was found cut into the top of one of them. The canopies, now very ruinous, of two of the original south aisle sedilia can be seen outside the south door. There was some controversy in 1926 when another piece of the original sedilia was presented to the Cathedral of St John the Divine in New York. A further gift to a church overseas was wood from the old nave roof, which was taken to New Zealand to be turned into wardens' wands in Wellington Cathedral, as an inscription on one of them records.

The door in the south wall of the aisle is the bier house door, which opens to the building outside, across the churchyard, which was once fitted out as a chapel where coffins could rest before being brought into the church for the funeral service. This door was renovated in 1928 as a memorial to George Arbuthnot, though it was noted at the time that his main memorial was to be found in all the work that had been carried out on the church during his incumbency.

Borne on the bier with white and bristly beard.

(SONNET 12)

The Burman monument

The large memorial tablet on the south wall of the south aisle is a monument to the (almost) last members of the Burman family of Shottery and Stratford who were prominent citizens of the town for at least 300 years. The earliest record of the family relates to John Burman, who is recorded in 1467, during the reign of Edward IV, as holding a tenement and a virgate of land here. Further mentions of the name occur during the reigns of Henry VII, Henry VIII and Edward VI, and from 1538 onwards, when it became mandatory for parishes to maintain records of births, marriages and deaths, Burmans were a constant presence. Between 1558 and 1662, 123 Burmans were baptised in Holy Trinity, forty-seven were married there and sixty-five buried. They were, moreover, prominent and active members of the church, with several of them serving as churchwardens and frequently attending vestry meetings.

Their link with the Hathaways was very close. One of their properties in Shottery, still known as Burman's Farm, was right next door to the Hathaway farm and the cottage now known as Anne Hathaway's. Stephen Burman was appointed by Richard Hathaway, Anne's father, as the executor of his will, along with Fulke Sandells who was one of those who offered sureties in the bond of Anne's marriage to William Shakespeare. Richard Burman was a witness to the will. At a later date Stephen's son, also called Stephen, was one of Anne's brother Bartholomew Hathaway's executors, along with Shakespeare's son-in-law, John Hall.

Richard Burman's second son, another Richard, was not one of the more upstanding members of the family, at a time when his cousins, Stephen and Clement, were devoted members of the church and frequently served as churchwardens. This Richard's wife, Ann, was fined for recusancy in 1592, and again some years later when she was a widow. Richard himself was fined for making a muckheap in front of his house in Church Street in Stratford, and he also defaulted on the church levy, which must have caused his cousins much mortification. Before his death he was made to turn over all his assets to his son, who was charged with paying off his debts, including money owed to Thomas Nash, Shakespeare's granddaughter's husband.

Subsequent generations continued to be stalwart members of the church, serving as sidesmen and churchwardens; and John Burman became the first of the family to become mayor of Stratford in 1699. Stephen Burman's name appears on a plate dated 1695 on the chained bible which is still on display in the church. By this time the family had been awarded a coat of arms and were described as 'gentlemen'.

Hugh Burman, who was mayor of Stratford in 1744 and is memorialised along with his wife Hester and his family in the monument on the south aisle wall, was the last of the family to play a prominent part in the life of the town. As the plaque so poignantly records, three of his seven children died in their twenties and one aged thirty-four; only one of his offspring married, and there were no grandchildren. The words on the plaque 'Beneath this monument...' indicate that the family vault was under the floor of the south aisle, and this is borne out by other inscriptions recording family burials on the floor of the nave and the aisles.

The family continued to be associated with Holy Trinity, though living elsewhere, many of them still farming in Warwickshire. There is a later Burman vault near the north porch, along with plaques on the walls of the porch itself. The last of the family to be buried in this vault was Dr Thomas Burman, who married the widow of the vicar of Holy Trinity, John Clayton, and died childless in 1893.

John Burman Holtom

The hatchments in the north aisle

The hatchments that hang on the wall of the north aisle are those of the Clopton family. The term is a corruption of 'achievement', which in heraldry means the complete coat of arms of a family. Hatchments were produced specifically to be borne before a funeral procession and were laid up afterwards as a permanent memorial.

The two to the west are for husband and wife John and Frances Partheriche and represent the end of the Clopton family after almost 600 years. Ignoring all the decorative elements, it can be seen that the two coats of arms are the same, the only difference being that the husband's are carried on a shield and those of his wife on a diamond-shaped lozenge; the difference in shape was because women did not bear arms in the true meaning of the word as they did not fight battles. Frances was a Clopton and brought their arms to her husband's family when they married, as well as their lands. Not being a Clopton himself, her husband was not entitled to combine, or impale, these arms with his own but was allowed to place them at the centre of his own coat of arms as an 'escutcheon of pretence', a heraldic term meaning that he was entitled to pretend to them.

The single hatchment at the extreme right is for an earlier, male Clopton; and the helmet that hangs high up on the east wall of the aisle, in the Clopton Chapel, is another funerary symbol associated with one of the Cloptons. Such helmets were not intended to be worn, but were carried in the funeral procession, like the hatchments, and then deposited in the church.

Bill Hicks

For his passage,
The soldiers' music and the rites
of war
Speak loudly for him.

(HAMLET, 5.2)

The stained glass in all the aisle windows was installed between 1897 and 1909, mostly as family memorials paid for by donors, though one in the north aisle was the gift of Sunday School children who had collected money for it. Two of the windows in the south aisle are the work of the noted artist C E Kempe, as is the 'poets' window' depicting Caedmon, Chaucer and Milton, in the north-west corner of the church, now within the shop; the two south aisle windows bear Kempe's signature, a tiny green wheatsheaf.

Opposite:
The poets' window.

Cædmon monacha
Geoffrey Chaucer
Ioannes Milton
A. M. D. G.

The Clopton Chapel

Hugh Clopton declared in his will, made just before his death:

> If it fortune me to decease upon Stratford upon Avon or in that country, then my body shall be buried in the parish church of the same. I will that my body be brought of ground with four torches and four tapers and no more. I will that the priests of the college and of the guild in Stratford upon Avon sing placebo and dirige with other orisons accustomed after Salisbury use, and mass of requiem for my soul every day for a month if I be buried there.

His tomb at the right of the chapel that now bears his family name carries his arms, those of the Mercers' Company, of which he was a member, and those of the City of London. However, it did not 'fortune him' to die in Stratford, but in London, in 1496, where he is buried in the church of St Margaret Lothbury. The tomb he intended for himself remains empty.

The splendid tomb on the left of the chapel is that of William Clopton, grandson of the William who had inherited Hugh Clopton's estate in 1496, and Anne, his wife. The effigies show a gentleman in armour, with his sword at his right and his head resting on a helmet; his lady wears a ruff and long gown with a pomander ball on her chest. The rubric running around the top of the tomb records that he died in April 1592 and she in September 1596.

Opposite: Hugh Clopton's empty tomb.

Below: The tomb of William and Anne Clopton.

The effigies of William and Anne Clopton's seven children; those in swaddling clothes died in infancy.

Hugh Clopton (*c* 1440–96)

Hugh Clopton was a great benefactor of Stratford, using his considerable wealth to build the nave of the Guild Chapel and the bridge over the River Avon, which still bears his name and still carries traffic today. He left in his will an unspecified amount, as well as detailed instructions, for the completion of work on the Guild Chapel, and also £50 for the cross aisle in Holy Trinity. He also built what he called his 'great house', New Place, the second biggest house in Stratford, which was later to be owned by William Shakespeare.

A younger son, he made his fortune in London, where he served as Lord Mayor in 1492. Contrary to later repute, he was not knighted, and described himself in his will as 'citizen, mercer and alderman'. He never married, and his heir was his great-nephew William.

Although much of his life was spent in London, he must have travelled frequently between there and Stratford, since he left a further £50 in his will, together with other moneys (including a third of the residue of his estate), for the mending of perilous bridges and ways within ten miles of Stratford; presumably he had intimate knowledge of the hazards they presented. It is clear that he never forgot his home town: even at the point when he was about to take up his role as Lord Mayor of London, he had to travel from Stratford to London to assume office; a body of aldermen of the city was sent ten miles beyond its walls to escort him there.

The 'sumptuous new bridge and large of stone' is perhaps his greatest legacy. John Leland rode over it on his way from Warwick: 'In the middle be six great arches for the main stream of Avon, and at each end certain small arches to bear the causey, and so to pass commodiously at such times as the river riseth'. The previous bridge, he says, was 'very small and ill, and at high waters very hard to pass by'. Trade improved after the bridge was built – previously 'there was but a poor bridge of timber and no causey to come to it, whereby many poor folks and other refused to come to Stratford when Avon was up, or coming thither stood in jeopardy of life'.

The borough clearly appreciated it. Later maintenance of Clopton's bridge was entrusted to wardens elected annually, with revenue derived from various small properties given or bequeathed for the purpose.

View of the Avon c 1932, with the Clopton Bridge in the background.

The tomb of George and Joyce Carew.

A rare addition to their tomb is the wall-piece above it, where can be seen their seven children, three of whom died in infancy and are therefore depicted in their swaddling clothes. They were Elizabeth, Ludowicke (both of whom died), Joyce, Margaret (who both survived), William (who died), Anne and William (who both survived). Their only living son was therefore their last born, but he died young, as did Margaret, and the estate passed to the only two surviving daughters, Joyce and Anne. It was their eldest daughter, Joyce, who was to ensure both that her parents' tomb retained its splendour and that she and her husband would also be buried in Stratford and memorialised in the Clopton Chapel.

Joyce's own tomb against the east wall of the chapel, where she is buried with her husband George Carew, is regarded by many as one of the finest Renaissance monuments in Europe. According to the inscriptions in Latin on the tomb, theirs was a long and happy marriage – although the story goes that when her parents initially disapproved of the match the couple eloped. Her epitaph records that she was 'the most sorrowful widow of the dearest and best meriting man' and 'while he lived, for 49 years shared with him in hope of the most happy resurrection'. He died in London on March 27 1629, aged seventy-three; she lived to the age of seventy-eight and died in 1637. Their only son predeceased them.

George Carew had a distinguished career under three monarchs, and became Baron Clopton and Earl of Totnes. He was King James I's Master of the Ordnance, and the front panel of their memorial shows the cannon, cannonballs, flags and barrels of his profession. Above lie the effigies of the earl and his wife, coroneted and in all their splendour, surmounted by a canopy.

Opposite: Pre-Reformation glass in the upper lights of the north window of the Clopton Chapel.

Below: Details of the Carew tomb.

The grandeur of the Carew/Clopton tombs is balanced in this chapel by a small plaque on the wall to the right, between the Carews and the empty tomb, which pays tribute to the loyalty felt by a 'waiting gentlewoman' for her mistress and the affection which she received in return. Here is commemorated Amy Smith, who had served Lady Carew for most of her life and had expressed her deep desire to be buried at her mistress's feet. Though she died in Nonsuch in Surrey, Lady Carew honoured her wish and brought her body back to Stratford to be buried in the church where she herself would later be laid to rest. The plaque is surmounted by a coat of arms showing three greyhounds, which suggests that Miss Smith was perhaps a member of a 'gentle' family who had fallen on hard times, hence her attachment to Lady Carew's household.

The top lights of the glass in the north window of the Clopton Chapel, above the tomb of William and Anne, are pre-Reformation in date and are almost certainly part of the chancel glass, which in 1790 was described by Wheler as 'confusedly put together in the centre of the east window'. It was removed at the end of the nineteenth century and reinstalled here. The lower lights, with figures of Faith, Hope and Charity, were presented in 1902 by Sir Arthur Hodgson, then owner of Clopton House, in memory of his late wife.

An echo of the medieval devotions that were paid in this chapel is to be found today in the little statue of the Virgin Mary with the infant Jesus which stands on a small column at the head of Hugh Clopton's tomb. It was presented to Holy Trinity in the 1950s by St Gregory's Catholic church.

Above Amy Smith's monument is a plaque dedicated to Thomas and Eglantine Clopton, who died within a year of each other in 1643 and 1642, leaving two sons. Eglantine was a common Warwickshire name, after the sweet briar that grows there in profusion:

> I know a bank where the wild thyme blows,
> Where oxlips and the nodding violet grows,
> Quite over-canopied with luscious woodbine,
> With sweet musk-roses, and with eglantine.
>
> (*A Midsummer Night's Dream*, 2.1)

On the north wall to the left of the window is the monument of John and Barbara Clopton, with an inscription which records that they had six sons and four daughters, though when John died, in December 1692 aged forty-seven, only five of his children were alive. Barbara lived on until 1719 and was eighty years old when she died. Their son Hugh had the plaque erected, and Hugh's wife Elizabeth is also commemorated in the chapel: 'sprung from a most famous family, she increased their dignity as much by the beauty of her person as her virtues of her mind'; she died aged forty-two in 1721. Barbara Clopton's parents, Sir Edward Walker, Garter King of Arms, and his wife, Agnes, are also commemorated here, under Elizabeth Clopton's plaque on the east wall to the left of the Carew tomb.

Faith
Hope

CAUTION VERY LOW DOOR
GUIDES

Above and above right: One of the sites of a holy water stoup; and the vaulted ceiling in the north porch, showing the mutilated roundel.
Opposite: The inner doors of the north porch, with the thirteenth-century closing ring.

The north porch

The two-storey porch dates to around 1485 and is credited to Thomas Balsall, as part of the work he carried out on the church during his long tenure as dean. The interior of the porch has its original tracery on the walls and stone vaulting on its ceiling with, in the centre, a figure surrounded by a 'glory' of radiating lines. This was probably a depiction of the Holy Trinity, but in common with many of the other pre-Reformation sculptures in the church, it has been defaced; the chisel marks can still be made out.

The glass in the two little lancet windows in the east and west walls of the porch is Victorian: the one on the east side was installed in 1870 by the vicar, John Day Collis, in memory of his late wife, Josephine; the one on the west was placed there in 1879, as a memorial to Collis himself, by his second wife.

The outer doors – nearly sold for £1

The *Stratford Herald* of June 1 1894 reported that the outer doors of the porch had been nearly lost to the church only two weeks previously. They had been removed from their hangings two years before at the suggestion of the vicar, in order to reveal the ancient holy water stoups, and had been stored in a place of safety in case it was later decided to replace them.

A recent meeting of churchwardens had agreed to sell 'a quantity of old wood stored in the churchyard' for firewood, and a deal had been struck with a Mr Price. While inspecting the wood, he noticed the old doors and made an additional offer of £1 for them, which was accepted by Mr Humphriss, the churchwarden who was with him. Mr Price removed the doors that same evening 'not without some difficulty... due to the heavy weight, about 5cwt each'; but as he was doing so an alderman and retired churchwarden fortunately happened to be passing, noticed what was going on and raised the alarm. The vicar and the churchwardens met (without Mr Humphriss) and decided that the sale was 'entirely uncanonical and illegal'.

The leader in the newspaper pontificated on the subject: 'To prevent a similar piece of indiscretion in the future the doors should be rehung in their original positions. They ought, indeed, never to have been removed.' Mr Price, however, did rather well out of the deal; as the *Herald* further reported on June 8, the vicar and churchwardens had to pay him £3 to return them.

The east lancet window in the north porch showing Josephine Collis ministering to the poor and sick.

A story attaches to the porch west window. It seems that Robert Bell Wheler had in his possession some fragments of the original medieval glass from the chancel, which he passed on to his friend William Hunt, who in his turn sent them to the vicar. Collis and his wife installed them in the porch west window, but after Collis's death his second wife had this window replaced with her memorial to her late husband. Two years later, in 1881, William Hunt's son paid a visit to the church and noticed that his father's gift was no longer there. He investigated and found that that it was being kept without permission at the home of a church-warden. The Bishop of Worcester immediately ordered its restoration to the church.

The inner porch doors, opening into the north aisle, are the originals, installed when the porch was built and splendid examples of late fifteenth-century work. The outer doors conceal behind them, when they are open, the plinths for two large holy water stoups with carved stone angels above. The spaces in the wall are all that is left of the stoups themselves. The small integral door of the inner set of doors has a fine old closing ring, almost certainly thirteenth-century in date and older than the door itself. It is said to be a 'sanctuary knocker' – a ring that a fugitive had only to touch to claim a number of days' safety from the pursuit of the law. Church sanctuary was a feature of medieval justice, but did not apply to all churches; it was abolished in the early seventeenth century.

On the outside of the west wall of the porch can be seen a number of small hollows in the stone two or three centimetres in diameter. They have been there for a long time, and are thought to be either marks made by weapons being sharpened on the stone or holes left by bullets fired at people perhaps taking refuge in the churchyard during the Civil War.

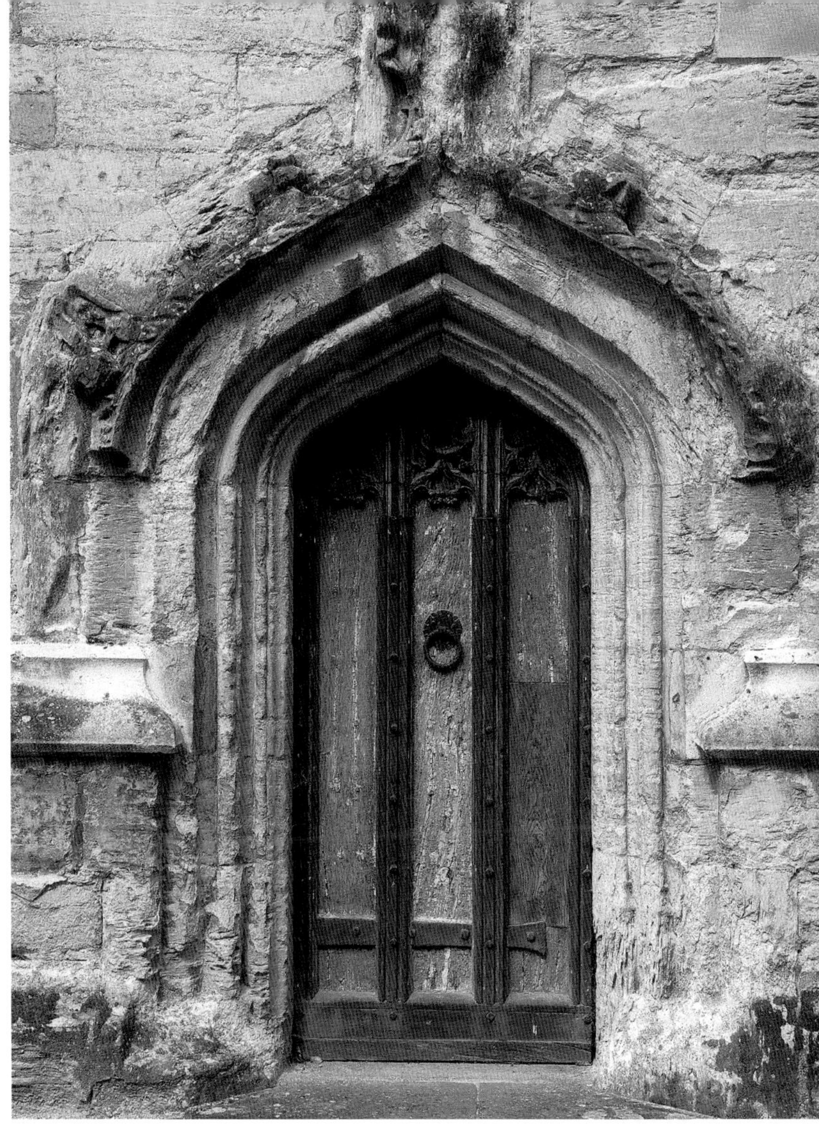

The exterior of the priests' door on the south wall of the chancel.

The chancel

Thomas Balsall completely rebuilt Holy Trinity's chancel in the 1480s, and although it has undergone many vicissitudes since then, it still remains much as he conceived it. The priests' door on the south wall, with its crocketed hoodmould above, is still in place, and the tracery of the windows is mostly intact. The now blocked up door on the north side also still has its elaborately carved – though now very damaged – hoodmould, showing St Christopher with the infant Jesus on the left and the Resurrection on the right.

The chancel is what is known as 'weeping'; it leans to the left, away from the line of the rest of the church, and has a rather larger deflection – five feet – than other examples. The fact that this is a not uncommon feature in medieval churches argues for its being deliberate rather than a response to a difficult site, and the most usual explanation is that it is meant to represent Christ's head falling to the side as he hung on the cross.

The name of Jesus

Devotion to the name of Jesus was the focus of a powerful spiritual movement in Thomas Balsall's time. It concentrated on Jesus's earthly life and on meditation, singing and prayer centring on his name; and the chancel of Holy Trinity still has many relics of that devotion. Knowing about it and recognising it helps both to bring the chancel to life and to remind us of how it looked and felt in Balsall's day.

He himself ensured that all the carvings on his tomb should reflect that devotion, showing as they did scenes from Jesus's life; the carvings around the door by Shakespeare's grave again show Jesus, being carried by St Christopher on the left and rising from his tomb on the right. All these carvings were mutilated at the Reformation, with his face being hacked off; but one beautiful representation of Christ's face still nestles untouched under the canopy of one of the medieval sedilia – unnoticed by today's visitors and by yesterday's religious police.

Balsall also built a new altar in the church, called the Jesus Altar, close to the door in the south-east corner of the nave that leads up to the ringing chamber in the tower. Here a special Jesus Mass was celebrated every week, usually on a Friday. Balsall had designed a showcase intended to reveal and celebrate the life of his Saviour. And a further clue reveals more. All around his tomb, easily overlooked, are the letters IHS, which can also be seen on Balsall's own seat in the misericords. They are the capital Greek letters for JES, the first three letters of Jesus's name.

Martin Gorick: Extract from sermon series 'Between two funerals', 2006

Above: Thomas Balsall's tomb.

Right: The original medieval font.

The monumental tomb that Balsall built for himself sits against the north wall within the sanctuary. This was once richly ornamented with brasses and stone carvings, but was mutilated when such ornamentation became regarded as idolatrous.

The chancel also contains the original medieval font in which Shakespeare was baptised, now much damaged. It was removed from the church in 1747, probably when a new font was commissioned (the font that is now to be found in the Guild Chapel). The original was taken to the house of the parish clerk in Church Street, and remained there in use as a water cistern or cattle trough until 1823 when it came into the possession of a Captain Saunders. The *Stratford Herald* reported on March 3 1861 that Mr William Hunt had purchased it in order to restore it to the church, and that it was safely deposited in the chancel a few days later. It was relined with lead and zinc in 1910, and was used for christening for several years. The current baptismal font, which stands at the west end of the nave, is a Victorian copy of this original.

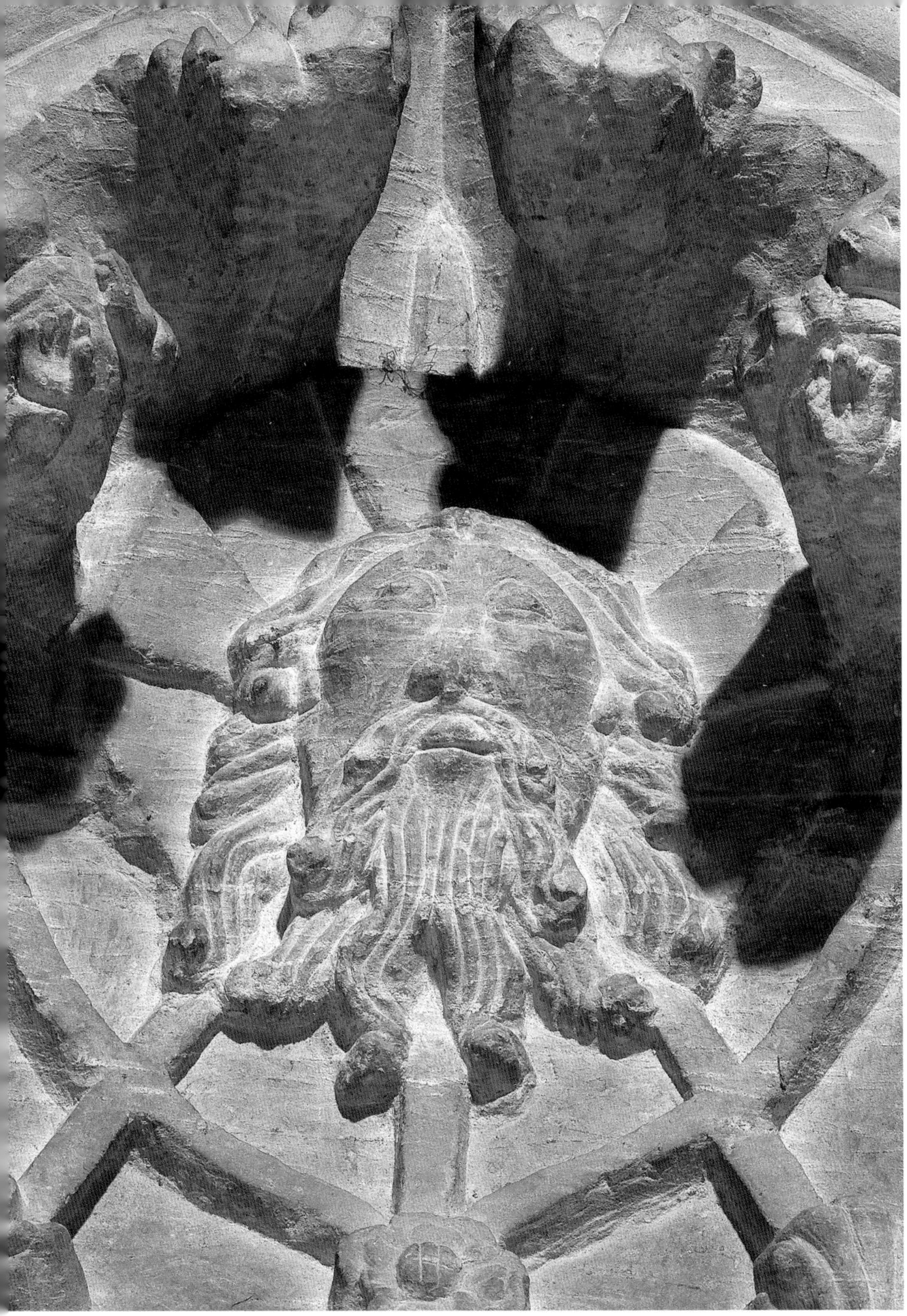

Left: The vernicle.
Below: Detail of the *mensa.*

A remarkable pre-Reformation survival is the *mensa*, or stone altar slab, which now sits on top of the Victorian altar but originally graced the chapel of St Thomas of Canterbury in the chantry in the south aisle. It was rediscovered beneath the floor there when the organ was being moved at the end of the nineteenth century, and had perhaps been deliberately hidden when changes in religious practice meant that it had to be removed; three of its original five incised crosses, representing the wounds of Christ on the cross, can still be seen.

Another survival can be seen in one of the three sedilia, the original medieval seats for the priests, on the south wall of the sanctuary. The two nearest the altar have carved Tudor roses under their canopies; but the third retains the face of Christ. This is unusual in a church where all other such representations have been systematically chiselled away. It may be a vernicle – a representation of Christ's face as it was miraculously transposed on to the cloth with which, in the Catholic tradition, St Veronica (hence its name) wiped his face as he carried his cross towards Calvary. And it appears to have attracted little notice for many years until Martin Gorick actually used the sedilium for its original purpose and sat in it during a service; when he glanced up he was somewhat startled to spot it. It was only then that its significance re-emerged.

GOOD FREND FOR
SAKE FORBEARE,
CLOASED HEARE.
WILLIAM

Opposite: The sanctuary.
Right: One of the angels on the reredos.
Below: Sanctuary floor tiles.

The altar was moved to a new position, standing out from the wall behind it, when major renovation works were carried out in the chancel in 1890–2. It was then that the *mensa* was placed in its current position; but not before the vicar had secreted within the new altar a lead box containing an account of the recent renovations and alterations to the church and the finding of the old altar table. The Purbeck marble steps were new at this time too, reflecting one of the tenets of the Gothic revival that required an ascent to the altar; and at the same time the floor of the sanctuary to the right and left was paved with what appear to be medieval tiles, though with some larger Victorian ones interspersed. The floor of the chancel itself was relaid with stone on a foundation of concrete, and pipes for heating were installed.

Mutilations

The fundamental changes in religious practice brought in at the Reformation had a massive impact on the appearance and decoration of churches and the form of worship that took place within them. The three decades between 1530 and 1560 saw waves of religious upheaval and confusion, as Henry VIII broke away from the authority of the Pope, his son Edward VI introduced the first English Protestant prayer books, his daughter Mary I reimposed Catholicism and her sister Elizabeth I finally moved back again to Protestantism.

It was perhaps during the early years of Elizabeth's reign that the deliberate mutilation of much of the Holy Trinity imagery occurred; though there was another phase of general destruction under the Commonwealth when strongly Puritan ideas prevailed, and it is not clear whether some of the damage at Holy Trinity might have occurred at this later time. In any event, the Protestant approach to worship moved away from the earlier Catholic practice, which relied on stories told through paintings, statues, stained glass and imagery generally to instruct the faithful and keep them obedient. The new method was to rely solely on the word of God, preached and acclaimed by his ministers in buildings stripped of what were now seen as idolatrous distractions from the simple truth.

All the trappings of the medieval church had to go: plate was melted down, stained glass smashed, the cult of the Virgin Mary suppressed, statuary daring to show the face of God destroyed. Altar tables changed too: the old stone ones reeked too strongly of sacrifice and blood; communion was now to be a shared meal, at a wooden table such as one might have in one's home.

At Holy Trinity these reforms resulted in the chiselling away of the faces of God and Christ wherever they were represented. The central boss in the porch ceiling suffered from this defacing, as did the images from the life of Christ on Thomas Balsall's tomb in the chancel and the carvings above the door in its north wall.

Above: St Christopher carrying the infant Christ, whose head has been chiselled off; the carving is part of the hoodmould over the old charnel house door in the chancel.

Left: The plain, unadorned whitewashed chancel in an 1827 engraving.

The new dispensation preferred plain glass in the windows; but some of the stained glass at Holy Trinity seems to have survived, since pre-Reformation glass is recorded as being in place in the middle of the seventeenth century, and was still there, though in a worn state, at the end of the eighteenth century. The finest surviving medieval stained glass is in the most inaccessible corner of the chancel, invisible from most of the church, which is surely no accident.

Whether the pre-Reformation survivals at Holy Trinity were the result of laziness or disaffection, it is tempting to speculate that at least some of those charged with carrying out the mutilations had their hearts less than wholly in the work. Perhaps it was just simpler to bury the *mensa* table of the altar of St Thomas of Canterbury beneath the floor, rather than smash it up entirely or reuse it elsewhere. But sparing the face of Christ in the chancel sedilium, where it sits half hidden and half in plain view, hints at a more deliberate decision.

John Shakespeare, William's father, was personally involved in these early Elizabethan religious upheavals, though there is no evidence that he had anything to do with the defacing of images in Holy Trinity. He was, however, as he noted in his accounts, responsible for paying out two shillings for 'defacing images in the chapel' of the Guild of the Holy Cross, where the frescoes were whitewashed over. He was also responsible, in 1564, when he was Acting Chamberlain of the Stratford Corporation, for taking down the rood loft in the chapel and providing seats for the minister and the clerk. Rather than being faced with a typical medieval array of narrative paintings to edify and frighten them – as the Doom fresco above the chancel arch was certainly meant to do – worshippers in the Guild Chapel now found themselves in a plain auditorium entirely devoted to preaching the word of God.

Left: The horned head-dress on a figure from misericord no 15.

Below: An angel armrest.

The misericords

Holy Trinity's misericords are among its glories. Not only are these choir seats in the chancel remarkable survivors of the pre-Reformation period but they are also full of fascinating religious imagery and reminders of social life 600 years ago.

Their name comes from the Latin *misericordia*, which means 'an act of mercy', and that is precisely what they were – clever seats designed to prop up the old and ailing, or merely tired youth, during the seven offices, as well as masses, at which the priests of the college were required to be present each day, and during which they had to stand for a great deal of the time. When in the down position, the hinged seats are straightforward choir stalls; but when the seats are turned up they provide small projecting mini-seats – the misericord seats – on which the occupants of the stalls could rest while still appearing to be standing.

The shape of the misericord seat is a good indicator of date; the earliest are simply semicircular, but they became more elaborate as time passed until in the fifteenth century they acquired the profile to be seen on the Holy Trinity examples – a moulded polygonal outline with a point in the centre. Further dating evidence is provided by the details of the costume worn by some of the carved figures; the horned head-dress to be seen on one of the seats, for example, was the height of fashion between 1430 and 1440.

The arm rests of the choir stalls are decorated with carved angels, their faces turned upwards in adoration. But it is under the seats that the most exuberant decoration is to be seen, in a place which was more often than not invisible. They must, however, be seen in the context both of medieval piety, when every aspect of a church must redound to the glory of an all-seeing and all-knowing God, and of the pride of the woodcarvers in their skill and ingenuity. They decorated the seats because they wanted to show off not only their talents but also their understanding of religious symbolism and their sense of humour.

A great deal of work and time went into the misericords; each stall seat was carved out of a solid piece of black oak, and the quality of both material and carving is still visible despite the inevitable ravages that six centuries have visited upon some of the work. Each seat carries three images: one at the base of the misericord seat itself and two others on either side. The images cover a whole range of human, animal and foliate motifs, though the symbolism is not always easy to interpret, and is remarkably wide-ranging, taking its inspiration from Christian literature and liturgy, ancient fables, popular romances, heraldry, scenes from everyday life and images of real and imaginary animals.

Carry his water to th' wise woman.

(*TWELFTH NIGHT*, OR WHAT YOU WILL, 3.4)

Left: Detail of no 16.

Below: Detail of no 22.

The major themes of Christianity – the fall of man, the struggle between good and evil, the magnanimity of Christ contrasted with the malevolence of the devil – are interspersed with images deriving from folk traditions, such as 'green men'. Some faces are benevolent while others are menacing or sinister – a protruding tongue was a gesture of defiance, and some faces portray fear in the constant presence of the grim demonic forces believed to be rampant in the world.

Mythical beasts often relate to one of the many bestiaries which sought to use animal imagery to illustrate Christian themes; the hunted unicorn, for example, on number 15 (see box, overleaf) was a symbol of the incarnation of Christ and his sacrifice for the sins of mankind: a powerful beast laying its head meekly in the lap of a maiden and submitting to capture.

Other images relate to everyday life. Number 16 has two apes, one urinating into a flask and the other looking at the contents – a jibe against the quack doctors of the time who made their diagnosis by examining their patients' urine.

Two others (numbers 25 and 26) show scenes of men and women fighting: number 25 has two such scenes, the one on the left showing a man grabbing a woman's hair while she tries to scratch his face while kicking him in the crotch, and the one on the right showing a grotesque half-woman half-animal being simultaneously attacked by a dog which is biting her leg and a man who is beating her with a birch. The central scene of number 26 is equally graphic: here a woman with an elaborate head-dress has grabbed a man by the beard and raises a saucepan to beat him with, while also kicking him. The violence of the scene is given added force by the fact that it is flanked on both sides by plaited roundels containing the sacred monogram IHS.

The graphic carvings on the misericords would have been among the most vivid images witnessed by the young William Shakespeare as he wandered around his parish church. In a provincial town where all wall paintings and religious statuary had been removed, they would have made a strong impression on any imaginative young boy. Did the lolling tongue of the scold and the vivid picture of a scold's bridle set up a chain of wondering that led to *The Taming of the Shrew*? Did the faces appearing out of flowers emerge in *A Midsummer Night's Dream*? They certainly would have formed part of Shakespeare's experience of worshipping in Holy Trinity, and their robust and fanciful imagery may well have played its part in fuelling the ideas that were forming in his head.

Right: Detail of no 25.

Left: Detail of no 26.

The choir stalls with their misericords were removed and repaired in 1890 as part of the work on the chancel done at that time. When they were replaced, they were raised on a new stone base intended to fend off dry rot; the small rose-shaped apertures in that stone base are presumably to aid air circulation, though it has also been suggested that they may have added an extra resonance to the singing. New seat backs were made at the same time, each one costing nine guineas and donated by people whose gifts are recorded in the inscriptions at their base. There are many prominent Stratford names to be seen in these inscriptions, whether of the donors themselves or of family or friends in whose memory the gifts were made.

The misericords are still in use today, perhaps most evocatively each month when the men of the choir sing the ancient plain chant service of Compline – one of the services the college of priests would have sung when the stalls were new.

Seat backs inscribed with donors' names.

Details of the misericords

Number 1 is the stall nearest to the altar on the northern, left, side of the chancel and they lead round to number 26 which is the one nearest to the altar on the southern, right, side.

1 A bearded man with an Eastern (Saracen?) headdress flanked by, on the left, a duck or goose and, on the right, an ostrich with a horseshoe in its beak; this refers to the legend that ostriches eat iron to improve their digestion

I'll make thee eat iron like an ostrich, and swallow my sword like a great pin, ere thou and I part.

(HENRY VI PART TWO, 4.9)

1

10

15

18

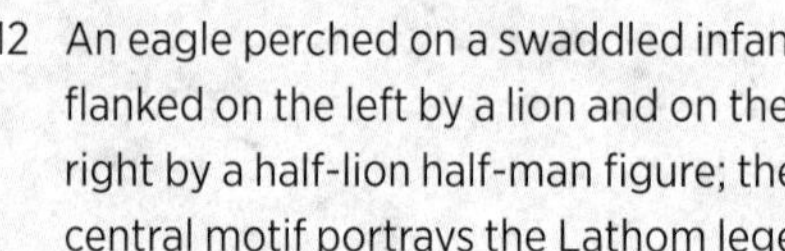

2 Foliage

3 Roses

4 An owl with outstretched wings, flanked by foliage

5 A rush basket containing the head of an animal, flanked by foliage

6 The central carving is damaged; hanging masks form the sidepieces

7 A lion with twin bodies and large ears, flanked by wyverns

8 Foliage

9 A camel with palm leaves, flanked by horned wyverns

10 A naked woman riding a stag, with flowers, trees and a scroll; foliage on either side; she may represent 'luxuria' or lechery

11 A mermaid and merman, flanked by foliage; she is combing her hair and holding a mirror

12 An eagle perched on a swaddled infant, flanked on the left by a lion and on the right by a half-lion half-man figure; the central motif portrays the Lathom legend, in which an infant was brought by an eagle to the aged Lord of Lathom who was childless and eager for an heir

13 A man and a woman rising from whelk shells, flanked by foliage; they are both holding distaffs and she also has a carding instrument

14 An eagle with supporting birds (hawks?) holding a coronet above its head, flanked by grotesque winged figures with, on the left, a woman's head, and on the right, a man's

15 The taming of the unicorn, an allegory of the Incarnation; a unicorn surrenders itself to a seated woman with a horned headdress, allowing itself to be captured by the hunter to the right; oak leaves and acorns flank the central image

16 Two muzzled and chained bears are flanked, to the left, by an ape examining a flask of urine and, to the right, an ape providing a specimen of urine into a flask

17 St George and the dragon; the saint is dressed in the armour of the period and has a palm tree to the left and a maiden kneeling in prayer to the right; the sidepieces are grotesques, with human heads, animal hindquarters and birds' feet

18 A satanic horned mask flanked by comic masks

19 A human face with ram's horns, flanked by a dolphin to the left and a goat to the right

20 The top half of a nude woman resting on her right arm, flanked by harpies

21 A foliate mask, flanked by a human head to the left and a monster's head to the right, both within a collar made of large leaves

22 Three female grimacers may represent the career of a scold; on the left she has her tongue out in mockery, in the centre she is grimacing and on the right she has been successfully gagged

11

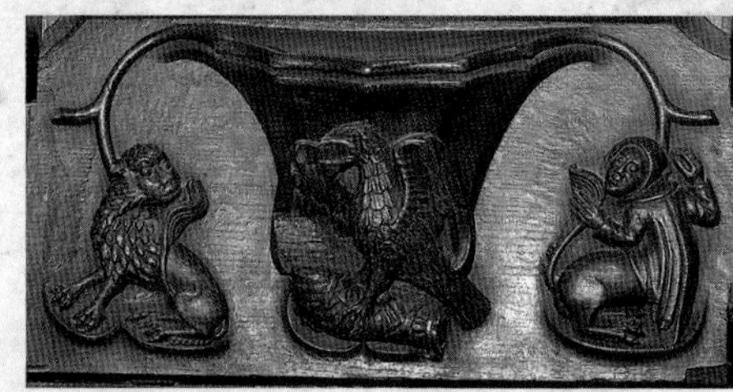

12

13

16

25

23 Foliage

24 Two serpentine bodies intertwined, one with a woman's head and one with the head of a monster; on the left a similar figures plays a pipe; on the right a man with a sword in one hand emerges from the mouth of a fish

25 A sphinx with a rider, flanked to the left by a man and woman fighting; he has seized her hair and she is trying to scratch his face while kicking him in the groin; to the right a half-woman half-animal figure is being beaten with a birch while her leg is attacked by a dog

26 A woman is pulling a man's beard and kicking him while raising a saucepan to beat him; the image is flanked on both sides by the sacred monogram IHS. This was the stall used by the dean

26

Displayed on the sanctuary walls are two other misericord seats, which originally came from the chantry chapel of St Thomas of Canterbury. One shows a seed sower and the other a twin-tailed mermaid with a mirror and comb; both are flanked by foliage.

Opposite: The monument of Richard Combe and Judith Combe.

Below: John Combe's effigy; note the missing foot.

Not marble nor the gilded monuments
Of princes shall outlive this powerful rhyme.

(SONNET 55)

The monuments in the chancel

Apart from Shakespeare's monument (discussed elsewhere; see pages 114ff), there are several significant monuments in the chancel, in the form of tombs, plaques and stained glass.

A plaque on the south chancel wall recalls James Davenport, vicar from 1787, who lived to the great age of ninety-two before dying in 1842. He had been simultaneously headmaster of King Edward VI School for a number of years. He is buried in the vault beneath the floor that was constructed for his wife, Margaret, who died at the age of thirty-six in 1796. Having lost his wife at such a young age, he also had to bury his daughter Margaret, who died aged eighteen in 1812, and his son James, who had taken holy orders but was only twenty-nine when he too died in 1821.

The monument on the north wall of the chancel, above Thomas Balsall's tomb, has the busts of Richard Combe and Judith Combe, his cousin and intended wife, and records the sad fact that 'she tooke her last leave of this life, the 17th day of August 1649, in ye arms of him, who most entirely loved and was beloved of her even to ye very death'.

Another Combe is buried in the large tomb in the north-east corner of the chancel. This was John, a friend of Shakespeare who died two years before him and left him £5 in his will. He also left the large sum of £60 for the construction of his tomb. His recumbent effigy – the work, like Shakespeare's monument, of Gheerart Janssen the elder, originally painted but 'stonewashed' in the eighteenth century – is dressed in a long gown and holds a book. The lengthy inscription starts with the words, 'Here lyeth

Left: The statue of St George, to the left of the east window. Note the fifteenth-century niche with the painted monster; the statue itself is late Victorian.

Opposite: Surviving pre-Reformation glass in the top lights of the window in the south-east corner of the chancel, showing Christ's Resurrection and Ascension.

interred ye body of John Combe Esqr; who, departing this life ye 10th day of July Ao Dni 1614 bequeathed by his last will and testament to pious and charitable uses…' and there follows a lengthy list of his bequests, some of which, as was the case with such arrangements during his life, carried instructions as to the interest that was to be charged on them. The inscription was never finished; and there is a tradition that the tomb also once carried a scurrilous verse penned by Shakespeare himself, which made merry with Combe's profession and reputation as a usurious money-lender:

> Ten in the hundred here lieth engraved
> A hundred to ten his soul is ne'er saved
> If anyone asks who lieth in this tomb
> 'O ho!' quoth the devil, ''tis my John-a-Combe'

Lieutenant Hammond, who described seeing Shakespeare's monument in the church during his travels in 1634, appears also to have seen these lines on Combe's tomb; as he noted in his account, Shakespeare 'did merrily fann up some witty and facetious verses', but 'time would not give us leave to sacke up', ie copy them. By 1673 they seem to have been removed. Robert Dobyns noted in that year that 'since my being in Stratford the heirs of master Combe have caused these verses to be razed so that now they are not legible'; he described Combe as 'a noted usurer'.

A further depredation to Combe's monument was partly repaired in 1896.The effigy had lost both its feet, probably to souvenir hunters; but in 1894 the vicar received a letter from a man who said that he believed he had in his possession one of the missing feet, which he would be happy to restore to the church. The stone was duly sent to Stratford and it was found to exactly fit the left leg, so it was replaced there. The right foot remains missing.

The tomb in the south-east corner of the chancel, which dates to 1751, is that of a J Kendall, a son who used his epitaph to pay homage to his father, who was Governor of 'Barbadoes' as it is spelled in the inscription. The niche above this tomb, as well as that on the north side of the east wall, still bears traces of its original paint. The figures now in them were placed there at the end of the nineteenth century; they represent St George and St Margaret.

The floor of the chancel was once covered with grave slabs, which now lie under the lozenge-shaped flags which were laid in the nineteenth century. But a few – in addition to the Shakespeare family graves – remain in the line of gravestones which are now protected behind the altar rail; here can be seen the grave slabs of 'Anne, wife of Francis Watts of Rine Clifford', and 'Francis Watts of Rine Clifford'.

Stained glass

Most of the stained glass in Holy Trinity is late Victorian. However, a few pieces of pre-Reformation glass survive, some in the very top lights of the window in the south-east corner of the chancel and a few more pieces which make up the top half of the window in the Clopton Chapel. Those in the chancel window probably represent the Joyful Mysteries of the rosary. In the apex is the Pentecostal dove, while another depicts Christ rising from the tomb and another shows the legs and feet of Christ rising heavenwards at the Ascension (right). These pieces of early glass are another of the church's great treasures.

Opposite: Watercolour of the chancel before 1835. Note the lack of an altar rail, though the measured plan of the chancel floor (page 81) includes it.

Right: The east window today.

Some of the chancel glass seems to have survived both post-Reformation and Commonwealth depredations, though by the end of the eighteenth century it was apparently in very poor condition. Wheler records that 'Time and accident… had so mutilated and damaged this glass that in the year 1790, at the alteration of the roof… the remains of it were taken out, and that which was preserved is now confusedly put together in the centre of the east window'. This was, he went on to say, 'all that was left of the glorious glass that once filled the windows of the chancel'. This arrangement of the east window can be seen in the watercolour painted sometime before 1835 (opposite) which shows the walls and ceiling of the chancel covered in whitewash and the windows glazed in plain glass, apart from the middle light of the seven in the east window. It is this glass that is now in the Clopton Chapel.

Robert Bell Wheler

Robert Bell Wheler, the Stratford historian, is commemorated in four of the lights, depicting the raising of Jairus's daughter, in the second window from the east end in the south wall of the chancel. A polished brass plaque below the window reads, 'The above four compartments of this window were enriched by stained glass in memory of Robert Bell Wheler the historian of Stratford who deceased 1857 aged 72 years'. The other four lights in this window, showing the raising of Lazarus, were given in 1866 by Dr Clayton in memory of his father, the Revd John Clayton, vicar of Holy Trinity 1842–9.

Wheler was born at Avon Croft, Old Town, and lived there for his entire life with his two sisters; none of them ever married. He appears scarcely ever to have left Stratford, apart from once in 1812, when he went to London for a month at the time of his formal admission as a solicitor in the court of King's Bench. He and his sisters are buried in Holy Trinity graveyard with their father – the grave is marked with a double headstone just inside the main gates on the left.

The east window was not replaced until 1894, when the church authorities were despairing of being able to raise enough money for it before an individual donor came up with the whole amount needed, £600. It represents 'The Adoration of the Crucified'. The first window at the altar end of the chancel on the south wall, of poor quality and depicting the four evangelists, is the Masonic window, dedicated in 1862 'in memory of William Shakespeare by his brethren of the Bard of Avon Lodge no 778'. There was a belief among some freemasons in the nineteenth century that Shakespeare had been one of them. Third from the east on the north side is another American window to add to the one in the south transept, depicting Shakespeare's Seven Ages of Man through personalities taken from the Scriptures. The cost of this one was defrayed by twelve years' worth of offerings from American visitors. The stained glass round the Shakespeare monument was given in memory of J O Halliwell-Phillipps, Shakespearian scholar, a great collector of facts and documents about the poet, a leading figure in the purchase of New Place for the Corporation and an instigator of the Shakespeare Museum.

Detail of the chancel ceiling.

NINETEENTH-CENTURY RENOVATIONS

By the early decades of the nineteenth century, Holy Trinity was showing its age. Moreover, Victorian ideas about church architecture and worship were beginning to dictate major changes to the layout and decoration of ecclesiastical buildings, changes which were underpinned by the technological advances of the time and funded from the profits of empire. Fashions had changed too; the church portrayed in the pre-1835 watercolour (page 76), with its plain whitewashed walls and ceiling, its unadorned glass and its choir stalls without backs or canopies, was not in keeping with the tastes of Victorian congregations. By the end of that exuberant century, Holy Trinity church would look very different.

In the 1830s the deteriorating state of the chancel was giving great cause for concern. A levy of 17s 6¼d in the pound had been raised in 1790 from the tithe-holders who were responsible for its repair, but by 1835 it had 'a broken, noxious and wet floor, with foundation walls gradually mouldering with the green damp from neglected drainage – timbers mildewing and rotting – limewashed walls – a flat, plastered ceiling; and the whole presenting a scene of tasteless patchwork and miserable economy' (*Warwick Advertiser*, April 29 1837). It is little wonder that the committee in 1835 wanted to 'restore the ancient roof and painted windows, to clean the walls of all whitewash and to secure the foundations of the chancel'.

The vicar, James Davenport, despite being eighty-five years old, involved himself in the vigorous fundraising that was necessary to undertake the repairs, and was happy to exploit the Shakespearian connection in seeking funds: 'It is intended to organise a Committee in the Metropolis, to cooperate with that of Stratford on Avon, and thereby to obtain an adequate sum of money from the admirers of Shakespeare to render his monument a building of stability, security and beauty, worthy, at once, of the Bard and of the present age, and competent to excite the admiration of succeeding generations.' The result was a long list of London patrons and subscribers. Among the other fundraising initiatives was the opportunity for 'noblemen and gentlemen of the county' to have their arms represented on the new medieval-type wooden roof on payment of a fee ranging from five to twenty-five guineas.

These efforts raised £1196 13s 11d, out of which George Hamilton was paid £1195 5s 'for new roof, altar railings, floor and other work executed in the chancel' and Mr Edkins £10 for a new cross. There was clearly still a shortfall in the money needed, so the church was forced to levy a church rate, which they knew would cause controversy. Every ratepayer was legally a member of the Established Church, but many dissenters objected and – in this case as in many

Detail of the St George window in the west end of the south aisle.

others – refused to pay such levies. In July 1837 four prominent local dissenters were summoned, including James Cox, a Baptist, who argued forcefully that he should not be forced to support a church he did not use. However, the magistrates decided in favour of the imposition of the rate, and when the dissenters still refused their goods were sequestrated.

A large watercolour painting by Charles Barber, still in the possession of the church, shows the arrangement of the body of the church prior to 1839. At that time the chancel was inaccessible to the congregation, and the tower arch was mostly hidden by the large, mid-eighteenth-century organ and gallery, with a tall two-storeyed pulpit standing in the centre in front of the organ loft. On either side the aisles were filled with galleries and there were tall pews in front of the pillars of the nave, as well as seats in the centre for the poor. The candelabrum donated by Sarah Woolmer hung at the west end of the nave in front of the font, which is the one that had been commissioned in the middle of the eighteenth century, with a cover surmounted by a dove.

The later painting that now hangs on the west wall of the church depicts the next phase of Victorian renewal, which started in 1840 and cost around £4000. This shows a much more open and less oppressive arrangement. The organ was moved to the west end of the church, the high pews were replaced with low ones, there were new galleries in the aisles and a new pulpit was positioned against the south-west pier of the tower. The congregation could now see into the chancel, since the rood screen which formerly closed off the crossing was moved in 1842 to its current position across the arch to the north transept. The candelabrum too had gone; Bloom records it in 1902 as hanging in the north transept, from where it was

Above: Painting of the layout after the works of 1840.

Left: Painting by Charles Barber showing the arrangement of the nave prior to 1839.

The 1836 plan of the chancel floor

As a preliminary to the repair work carried out in the 1830s, a record was made of the inscriptions on the stones then forming the chancel floor. This document, which still exists in The Shakespeare Birthplace Trust's archives, is titled 'Stratford chancel. Plan of all the flags with inscriptions and the names of all the persons interred. Examined the 16th June 1836.' It is a methodical, measured plan of what could then be seen, though it doesn't transcribe everything. Some stones are marked just with the word 'Latin', and others are described as worn away, broken or blank. There are only three mentions of dates on the document, all later than Shakespeare's burial: 1699, 1746 and 1784.

The plan shows clearly that in 1836 the altar rail was positioned behind the line of gravestones which included those of the Shakespeare family, making the stones very vulnerable to the feet of visitors. It also depicts three rows of tiles between the gravestones of William and Anne Shakespeare. There is a space 3ft 3in wide between the heads of that line of graves and the feet of the nearest graves in the chancel; this space is empty apart from a flag with the words 'Ne Cesquissima'. As the plan also shows, the inscription on Susanna Hall's gravestone had been removed in order to allow for the name of Richard Watts of Ryon Clifford to be inscribed there. Her original epitaph was soon to be recut on her stone.

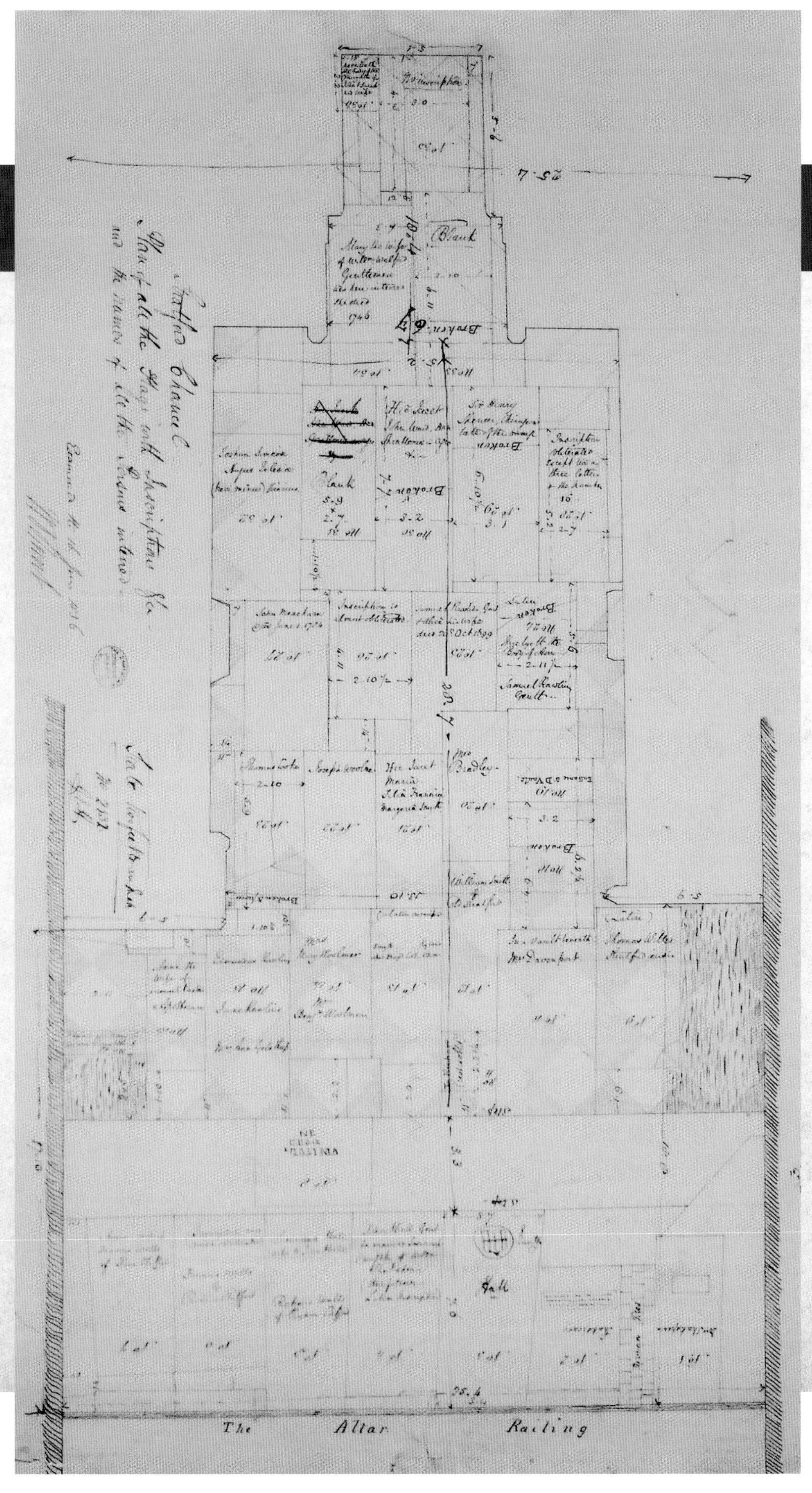

The chancel after 1838.

eventually moved to its current position in the crossing. And the font shown in the painting is the newly commissioned copy of the broken original, which was restored to the church in 1861 and placed in the chancel; the seventeenth-century font had been moved to the Guild Chapel.

All this work seems to have taken only a year or so, since the opening ceremony for the organ in its new position took place on June 9 1841 when there was a recital of Haydn's *Creation* with a large chorus and specially engaged solo singers. But the position of the organ appears to have been a source of dissatisfaction, since it was soon to be moved again, this time to the north transept; but this position too was problematic, because it blocked up the whole of the transept and half of its power was lost into the pillars of the tower and the heavy walls of the Clopton Chapel. So in 1889 it was once again repositioned, with part of it put in the chapel of St Thomas of Canterbury at the east end of the south aisle and the rest in a loft built for it over the arch under the tower. Its opening on the Eve of All Saints drew a large congregation, who joined vigorously in a rendering of the *Te Deum* which demonstrated its power. It remains in that position today.

The second half of the nineteenth century saw a great deal of repair and renewal, though Holy Trinity was more fortunate than other medieval churches in escaping some of the more zealous Victorian interventions. The spire was repaired in 1867, but by 1870 there was a warning that the bells could not be rung because their vibration caused pieces of plaster to fall from the tympanum over the chancel arch. All the records of repair to the fabric at this time show that iron clamps and rods were used to strengthen and pin the masonry, thus storing up major problems for the future.

By the time George Arbuthnot arrived as the new vicar in 1879, it was clear that a great deal of work was needed, and he was eager to put it in train. Within two months of coming to Stratford he established a parish magazine, and in the first issue he announced his intention of raising funds to renovate the church. But his plans did not always go smoothly, and he met what seems to have been vigorous opposition from some of his congregation. In 1882 a meeting in the Town Hall saw the vicar declaring that he would have nothing more to do with the restoration or repair of the church; but despite his high dudgeon, the committee that was formed to take the work forward refused to hand full control to him.

1903 repairs.

Recourse was had to the Society for the Protection of Ancient Buildings (SPAB), formed in 1877 by William Morris to counteract the destructive 'restoration' of ancient buildings being practised by many Victorian architects. SPAB suggested that George Frederick Bodley of the architects Bodley and Garner be asked to produce a report on the condition of the church. A leading exponent of the Victorian Gothic revival, he was one of the major ecclesiastical architects of the time. His recommendations were that the side galleries should be removed, the transepts opened up, a new vestry built and the organ moved. Apart from the new vestry, much of this was accomplished over the next decade.

Another phase started in 1890, mainly on the chancel which was closed off for two years; at the end of this time it had acquired much of its present appearance. There followed repairs to the Clopton Chapel, the installation of most of the stained glass windows and new heating. The excavations necessary for the heating apparatus exposed the old lower floor, which had been hidden by the 1840 work; inscribed stones were revealed, as well as a long row of arched brick vaults. When the work was done, the heating engineer guaranteed a constant temperature of fifty-five degrees inside the church when it was freezing outside. And when the builders pierced the wall in the south transept for the installation of new organ parts, they discovered a small thirteenth-century window 'in a very mutilated state'. Bodley, still the architect, advised that it was not worth preserving.

Bodley died in 1907, and was succeeded as architect by Guy Pemberton. He later made notes on the work that he had overseen during his tenure, which included underpinning the whole of the west front with reinforced concrete since it had been discovered that there were no foundations and that the walls went only nine inches into the ground. While doing this work quantities of ancient human bones emerged; as Pemberton noted, the surest way to heaven was to be buried under the very walls of a church. They were reinterred on the site of the charnel house. Work was also carried out on the aisle roofs, and the top eighteen feet of the spire had to be rebuilt after it was struck by lightning. The opportunity was taken to install a new bronze weather vane and to regild the ball at its foot; documents were put inside it to record the event.

Protecting Shakespeare's monument

Guy Pemberton: 'During the violent and stupid [*sic*] Suffragette movement a threatening letter was received by the vicar that they would come and deface as far as possible the bust of Shakespeare on the north wall of the chancel, just above his grave. How such an act could have enhanced their cause it is difficult to imagine, but we could not take risks so I had a steel case made with very light sections screwed onto wall brackets and glazed with the then quite new invention, Triplex glass. This case is detachable and when not required lives in the parvise over the north porch. At the same time it was considered desirable to make a glazed steel case to place over the register recording William Shakespeare's christening, also glazed with Triplex glass.'

The gold ball

Guy Pemberton recorded that the ball at the foot of the weather vane at the top of the spire was regilded during his tenure as church architect, but eighty years later this regilding was worn and damaged. The opportunity was therefore taken, while scaffolding was in place around the spire, to refurbish the ball, but it was decided simply to repaint it as there was no money available for the much more costly process of coating it with gold leaf.

But then Bill Hicks stepped in; a retired engineer who has served as churchwarden several times and has also acted as buildings warden for the recent major works, he offered to fund the regilding in memory of his wife, Gillian Hicks. When the gold was in place, Margaret Sweet, the associate minister, braved the climb to the top of the spire to bless the new work. So now the gold ball at the apex of Holy Trinity church once again shines out as a beacon over the town of Stratford and the surrounding countryside, in honour of a loyal and much-missed member of its congregation.

The gold ball before and after its restoration.

MODERN REPAIR AND CONSOLIDATION

The church architect from the late 1930s until 1956 was Francis Yorke. The scrapbook he kept on his work for Holy Trinity was recently presented to The Shakespeare Birthplace Trust by his granddaughter, and reveals the scale of repair that he believed would have to be undertaken over the next few decades. The stonework of the south clerestory, in particular, needed urgent attention; as the builders who inspected it in 1938 wrote to Yorke, 'We have hardly ever come across stonework in such a deplorable and dangerous condition as that of these clerestory windows'. As Yorke himself wrote in an article in the *Warwickshire Journal*: 'The church has always been well kept and perhaps it has been its neat and trim appearance which, until recently, disguised the fact that behind this veneer lurked in many parts the canker of decay… The whole range of the south clerestory windows … was found to be actually crumbling to dust, and pieces of masonry began falling into the nave… Portions of the stonework of all twelve windows on the south side, internally, as well as on the weather side, may easily be crushed in the hand…'. The great west window was also in urgent need of restoration: 'This window is in a parlous state,

One of the new grotesques on the south chancel parapet.

Repair of the chancel roof in 2009 and, inset, the parlous state of the main chancel roof beam.

insomuch that it is quite unsafe to rear a ladder against it, even for the purpose of necessary reglazing.'

Attitudes towards restoration had, however, noticeably changed in the half century or so since major works had last been carried out. Whereas in 1886 SPAB had reported that 'The pinnacles are gone from the parapet and we hold that it would be a great mistake to put new ones', as they believed the building looked better without them, now it was decided that they should be replaced. The well-meaning Victorian use of iron as the medium for pinning and strengthening the stonework had resulted in the masonry splitting as the metal corroded; now all the iron was to be replaced with non-ferrous metal. And above all, although new stone was needed where the old could not be repaired, 'this must be done as seldom as possible for new stonework, even if most carefully copied from the medieval work, can never look the same'.

Repair and consolidation go on all the time. The first decade of the twenty-first century at Holy Trinity has seen three major programmes of work under the vicar, Martin Gorick, much of which has been funded by the Friends of Shakespeare's Church, a registered charity which came into being in 2003. The first phase dealt with the south wall and parapet of the chancel, where water had been running down inside, behind the misericords; work was done to consolidate the roof above, which had been damaged by dry rot and death watch beetle, and new grotesques were commissioned. A new cross was also commissioned for the apex of the east wall of the chancel. This is popularly known as Beryl's cross, in memory of Beryl Winter, a stalwart of the congregation who continued as a bellringer into her eighties; what remains of the old cross can be seen set into the ground near the east end of the bier house. The next phase involved extensive work on the

Friends of Shakespeare's Church

At the start of the twenty-first century Holy Trinity church was in a parlous state. Although diocesan inspections had revealed that much needed to be done, no major repair and consolidation projects had been undertaken for decades. Since the Reformation, the very considerable assets of the medieval college and guild had not been available in any significant manner to fund such repairs, but had been managed in a separate charity not linked to the church, 'for the benefit of the town'. Then at the turn of the twentieth century the Charity Commissioners agreed to funds moving into a re-formed charity, the Stratford Town Trust. The objects of the new charity now included the support of heritage and religion in the town.

The new Town Trust, keen to fulfil its new objectives, offered an initial grant of £20,000 to Holy Trinity church to enable it to found a new charity with objects solely related to the restoration and rebuilding of the fabric of the church. This new charity would have as its main aim the raising of funds and the channelling of them to the church to support repair work. The result was the establishment of the Friends of Shakespeare's Church, and early in 2003 charity status was achieved. The Town Trust has continued to support the Friends with offers of grants, sometimes tied to a matched funding condition. With this support, nearly a million pounds has been raised and spent upon major projects in the last seven years: the south chancel parapet and roof, the tower and the spire, the north clerestory and, most recently, the main beam of the chancel roof.

The Friends raise money in a variety of ways: a membership scheme, fundraising events in the church and the town, individual donations, appeals such as 'sponsor a window' and grants from any number of grant-giving bodies to whom constant recourse is had. Many members of the acting fraternity are active supporters, and offer their influential presence at events such as fundraising recitals. Dame Judi Dench and Sir Patrick Stewart are among the patrons and have both generously given of their time in this way. At one Shakespeare Birthday luncheon, Sir Donald Sinden closed the proceedings by urging all those present to 'open your pockets' in support of the church. All sorts of initiatives can bear rich fruit. A newspaper article about the dire straits the church is in, which was syndicated all over the world, resulted in outpourings of support and help. The donations are sometimes very small, but all are heart-warming and encouraging.

The church will continue to need the help of the Friends for the foreseeable future. There is a great deal of work still to be done to protect and maintain this fragile medieval building for generations to come. The next project for which fundraising is planned is consolidation of the Shakespeare family gravestones in the chancel, which are crumbling and damaged; and it is already clear that this initiative will provoke a great deal of debate.

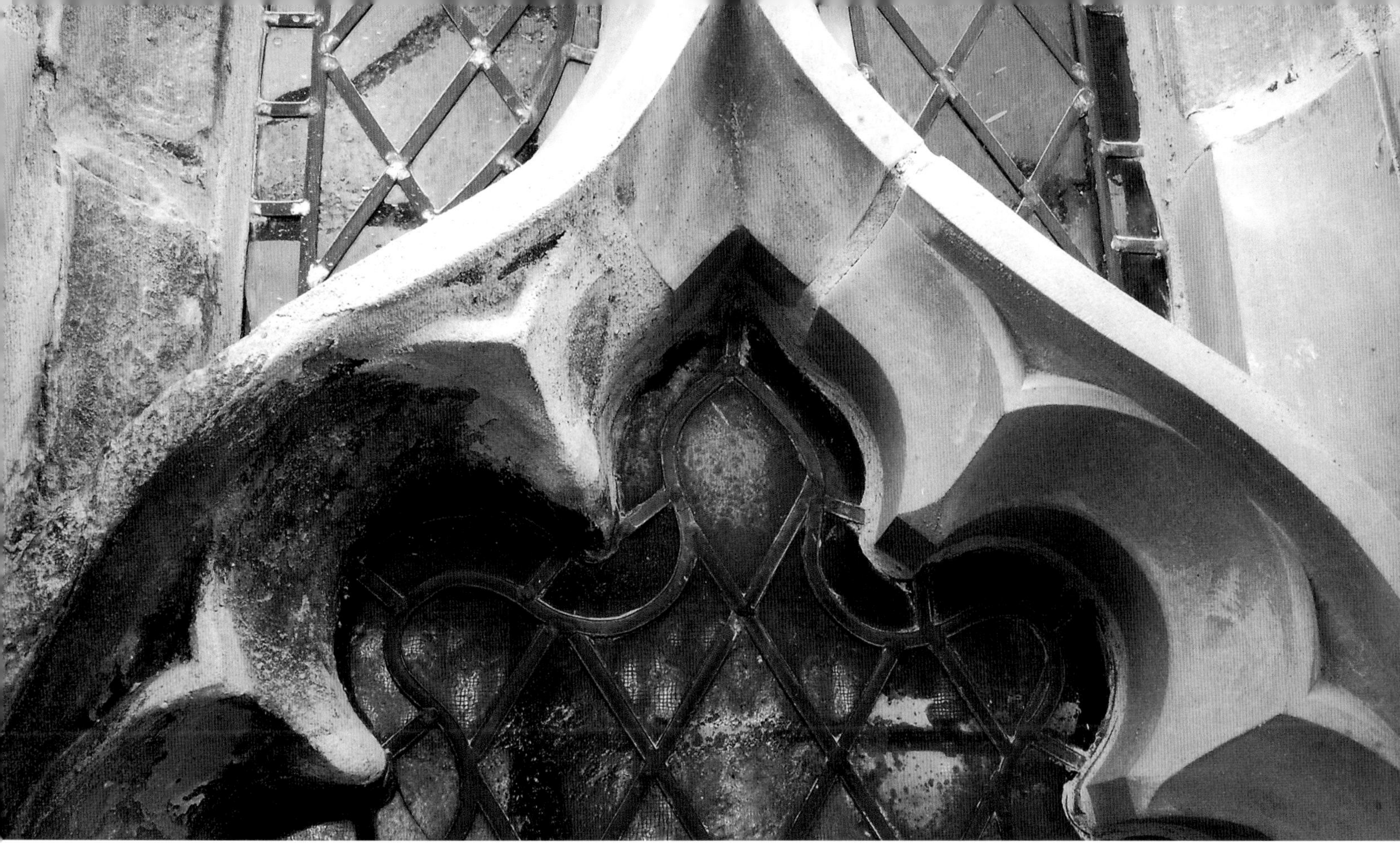

Restoration of part of the north clerestory window tracery.

tower and the spire. The inverted bowl of brick, built in the eighteenth century to support the new spire erected at that time, was collapsing and the nineteenth-century iron clamps were corroding and shattering the stone, so the ironwork was replaced, the brick shored up and the whole tower and spire repointed. One of the corner gargoyles on the tower was also replaced during this phase.

The 2009 phase of work involved the repair of the north clerestory, which was showing the same sort of dilapidation as had the south clerestory seventy years before, as well as work on the south aisle and chancel roofs – during which it was revealed that the main beam of the chancel roof was dangerously rotten, and extra urgent repair work had to be undertaken.

A building 800 years old will always need cherishing. Modern attitudes towards ancient buildings are arguably more enlightened than those of the past, when the old could be stripped away with impunity to make way for the new. But a church is also a living, working building that must meet the needs and wishes of those who use it – and today's clergy and congregations are able and willing to balance their own modern requirements with the venerable history of the building that sits so firmly at the centre of the lives of its community, and to recognise that they are merely its current custodians. Francis Yorke put this very well, fifty years ago:

> A church like this at Stratford holds in its old stones the spirit of the ages. It does not require a very long flight of the imagination while musing its inspiring precincts to conjure up the pageantry of the past. One may readily and vividly picture its once more colourful interior, its several consecrations, its masses and services, its changing music and song, its richly robed ecclesiastics, its long line of clerics and clerks, and its worshippers changing with the times in customs and character. In this most stately edifice once moved the quaintly clad men and women of the Middle Ages. There might once have been seen the richly ruffed folk of the Elizabethan age, succeeded by the Georgians, in gay skirted coats and hoops, and later the Victorians in their more sober attire, but with most subtly shifting crinolines. All these carried on the great tradition, living in faith and little recking of what today might mean. Here they congregated to pray in times of war, pestilence or famine, and here they met to offer thanksgiving for victory, health and harvest. It was these people who preserved for us what we have, who bequeathed to us what we hold. It is for us who succeed in our day and generation to take our place and part in the pageantry.

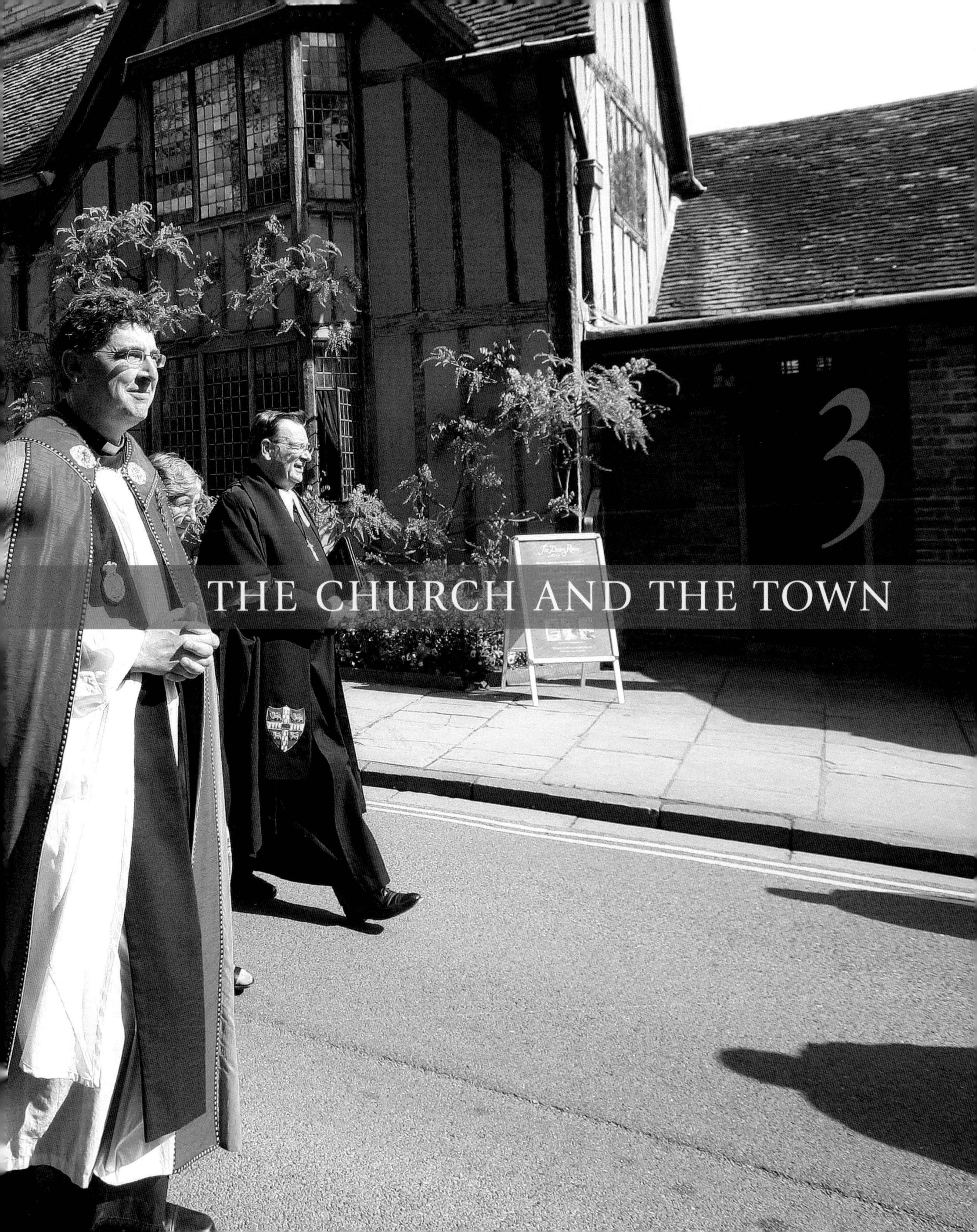

3

THE CHURCH AND THE TOWN

I'll give my jewels for a set of beads,
My gorgeous palace for a hermitage,
My gay apparel for an almsman's gown,
My figured goblets for a dish of wood,
My sceptre for a pair of carvèd saints.

(*RICHARD II*, 3.3)

Stratford's position, on an important crossing of the River Avon where several routes converged, was the foundation of its prosperity, underpinned and enhanced by the grant to the town in 1196 of the right to hold a market. Then, as now, it was a bustling place; but whereas today much of the town's economy centres on the theatre, the Shakespeare tourist industry and the retail and hospitality outlets that cater for those activities, in medieval and early modern times its fortunes were based on its proximity to the rich cereal-growing farmlands of south Warwickshire. This resulted in Stratford becoming a centre of the malting industry – the treatment of grain for use in brewing.

But its status as a market town meant that it was also the hub of the local area, the place to which farmers and traders from the villages round about brought their wares to sell, and the place where, in turn, they could buy the services and staples they needed. The town would have been particularly busy on Thursdays, market day; and the range of activities taking place is still evident in some of the surviving street

Left: View of Holy Trinity church from the roof of the Shakespeare Memorial Theatre, painted by W W Quartremaine *c* 1910.

Opposite page: Town meets church at the 2009 Shakespeare Birthday celebrations.

Virginia Woolf

All crabbers be damned – it is a fine unselfconscious town, mixed with eighteenth-century and the rest, all standing cheek by jowl. All the flowers were out in Shakespeare's garden. 'That was where his study windows looked out when he wrote *The Tempest*', said the man. And perhaps it was true. Anyhow it was a great big house, looking straight at the large stone windows and the great stone of the school chapel, and when the clock struck, that was the sound Shakespeare heard. I cannot without more labour than my road-running mind can compass describe the impression of sunny impersonality. Yes, everything seemed to say, this was Shakespeare's, had he sat and walked, but you won't find me, not exactly in the flesh. He is serenely absent-present; both at once, radiating around one; yes; in the flowers, in the old hall, in the garden; but never to be pinned down. And we went to the church, and there was the florid foolish bust, but what I had not reckoned for was the worn, simple slab, turned the wrong way, 'Good Friend for Jesus' sake forbear' – again he seemed to be all air and sun, smiling serenely; and yet down there, one foot from me lay the little bones that have spread over the world this vast illumination. Yes, and then we walked round the church, and all is simple and a little worn; the river slipping past the stone wall, with a red breadth in it from some flowering tree, and the edge of the turf unspoilt; soft and green and muddy, and two casual nonchalant swans. The church and the school and the house are all roomy, spacious places, resonant, sunny today, and in and out... – yes, an impressive place, still living, and then the little bones lying there, which have created: to think of writing *The Tempest* looking out on that garden; what a rage and storm of thought to have gone over any mind; no doubt the solidity of the place was comfortable. No doubt he saw the cellars with serenity. [...] And a good deal of parrot prattle from the old gramophone discs at the Birthplace, one taking up the story from the other. But isn't it odd, the caretaker at New Place agreed, [...] that all the rest, books, furniture, pictures etc, has completely vanished? Now I think Shakespeare was very happy in this, that there was no impediment of fame, but his genius flowed out of him, and is still there, in Stratford. They were acting *As You Like It*, I think, in the theatre.

Virginia Woolf, *Diary*, May 9 1934

names: Sheep Street, for one, and Rother Street, after the Old English word for cattle. Bridge Street boasted four inns, the Swan, the Bear, the Crown and the Angel, and was divided by Middle Row into Fore Bridge Street and Back Bridge Street. This was probably the busiest part of town, a little hive of industry with its smithies, taverns, butchers' shops, bakeries, haberdashers and shoemakers.

Stratford was famous for its fairs, which centred round religious feasts, including the eve of Trinity Sunday and the two days following, in honour of the dedication of the church, plus two in honour of the Cross – the Eve, Day and Morrow of the Exaltation of the Cross (September 14–16) and the Day and Morrow of the Finding of the Cross (May 3–4). By 1553 the two fairs honouring the Cross were the only ones remaining. However, the medieval hiring fair known as the Mop Fair, which was first given its royal charter by Edward VI, is still to this day held in early October, taking over the streets of Stratford with funfair rides, stalls and tents. Its original purpose was to provide a market-place for workers offering their services for the following year. They would advertise their skills by carrying the tools of their trade – a shepherd his crook, a maidservant a mop or broom, for example. Once hired, they would wear bright ribbons instead. Today's fair no longer has the aim of finding work for the unemployed, but is still opened by the mayor, who is led round it by the Mop Master, and still offers the opportunity for the townspeople to let their hair down and enjoy themselves, just as their predecessors did.

Stratford now is home to some 25,000 people; in Shakespeare's time it would have been a tenth of that figure at most, with fluctuations in times of famine or plague or when particular hardships caused a drift from the countryside into the town. The malting industry was a mixed blessing, in that its reliance on a process involving heat resulted in several disastrous fires that wiped out large swathes of the town – three times during Shakespeare's lifetime alone.

The shift of the town centre a little way away from its original site around the parish church was emphasised when Hugh Clopton's new stone bridge over the River Avon, about half a mile upstream from the church, replaced earlier wooden bridges in the late fifteenth century. But despite rivalries with the Guild Chapel, Holy Trinity remained the focus of the religious activities of the townspeople: regular worship, special feast days, baptisms, marriages, funerals and

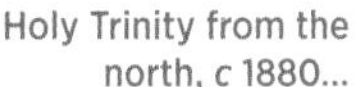

Holy Trinity from the north, *c* 1880...

the administration of ecclesiastical justice. Churchgoing was central to people's lives and sometimes a matter of obligation rather than choice. The church was also the place where much of life went on – one of the town's important meeting places, where deals could be done, social intercourse conducted and gossip exchanged. This relationship between church and town persisted for centuries, and has only recently, perhaps, become less marked with the decline in the second half of the twentieth century of regular religious observance – though Holy Trinity has resisted this trend, and enjoys weekly congregations numbering in the hundreds.

The vicar and the gossips (as recounted by Ursula Bloom)

...Soon the bells of the Holy Trinity church would start; it was Sunday evening, and six-thirty was Evensong... Naturally everybody went to church; it was imperative, a duty none broke, and to keep away would have been frowned on by the Reverend George Arbuthnot, the vicar. Church was a social duty; besides, friends met there, walking home afterwards and talking. Always in small towns there was much to be discussed, and always the soupçon of scandal which could be so vastly entertaining. Oh yes, everybody went to church...

Everybody would be at church tonight, for word had gone round the town that Mr George Arbuthnot had said that he would make an announcement from the pulpit. Mr Arbuthnot dressed like a ninepin, in a frock coat which girt his protruding stomach, and the proper high hat of the period. He called a spade a spade, believed in long sermons, and no fidgeting in church. If he started a row, he made sure that it was a real row, and he always won.

For many weeks now the whole town had been aware of a scandal that was going on; there were always scandals in small towns, of course, and life would have been extraordinarily empty and dull without them... Mr Arbuthnot was middle-aged, he had in fact never been young. He had married Margaret

... and from the south, *c* 1882.

The novelist Ursula Bloom, daughter of Harvey Bloom, vicar of Whitchurch and historian of Holy Trinity, portrayed the closeness between the church and the townspeople in her memoir, *Rosemary for Stratford-on-Avon*, published in 1966 but set in 1901. Her account, presumably passed on to her by her father, of the facing-off of town gossips by the vicar, George Arbuthnot, is both a vivid description of a real event and an encapsulation of Stratford society at the beginning of the twentieth century (see box). It cannot help but force comparisons with the accounts of the medieval bawdy courts and the echoes of day-to-day Stratford life in Shakespeare's plays.

Evelyn, a frail lady of aristocratic lineage, addicted to the feather boa, and the highly embossed hatpins with which she skewered down her forward-tilted hats, then the mode. They had no children...

Stratford had been well aware of Mr Arbuthnot's interest in a girl called Betty Smith [the name is fictitious]. She was a big tall girl, now about nineteen years of age, and she had no people of her own. She was an orphan, one was told, and Mr Arbuthnot had very graciously taken her under his wing... Naturally the town had talked about Betty Smith and George Arbuthnot. The chatter was the conventional quip in the back streets where a woman in one garden pegged out her washing and discussed the matter with the woman next door, who was pegging out hers... Everybody knew about it. The Swan's Nest which stood on the other side of the Clopton Bridge laughed at it. In the Falcon it was the scandal of the hour. In the Dirty Duck in Waterside, men chuckled at it... Tonight there was to be an announcement about it. The good people were trooping along to Holy Trinity church pondering on what this could be. Surely Mr Arbuthnot could not climb up into his own pulpit and announce, 'I am the father of Betty Smith' or even more formidable, 'I am the lover of Betty Smith'! One thing was certain, it was that he would speak the truth as they all knew. Or possibly throw down the gauntlet of challenge, a method at which he was an expert.

There came the sound of the Clopton carriages approaching. The family in the first one, the servants following in the 'servants' bus', the women all black-bonneted, the men in number one uniform. They turned the

corner into Old Town, and rattled on towards the church... The trees were dripping slightly in the avenue which led to the porch... The church was almost full. It looked very beautiful with the candles all lit on the distant altar, for this church had always gone in for good showmanship. Soon now, from the green marble Helen Faucit memorial pulpit, Mr Arbuthnot would speak. *Soon!*

One had to suffer the whole choral evensong before George Arbuthnot got into the pulpit to preach. He stood there arresting all attention. You could have heard a pin drop in Holy Trinity church. Then he leant forward. He looked at them and his eyes were gimlets. Some malicious gossip had recently been brought to his attention, and this gossip was exceedingly repugnant to him. The moment had come when he had decided to challenge it... Mr Arbuthnot had a tale to tell, oh! He was prepared to face the music, if the town was ignorant enough to believe that there was any music here, and there was *not*. There never had been and there never would be. Wallop! Down came his fist on the shelf of the Helen Faucit memorial pulpit... He knew who had repeated it... 'I know and I challenge you. After this service, come to the vestry, and I will tell you the truth. If you have the effrontery to prattle behind my back, at least have the courage to face the truth tonight. *Tonight.* In my vestry after the service is over, I shall expect you to be there.'

Nobody went to the vestry. Not a single man jack of them, yet here were the gossips and the tittle-tattlers, everyone knew them... The quality left first, and did not hurry; the upper middle classes came next, then the lower, the tradesmen and the humble poor. Had the crisis failed? It looked like it, for malicious tongues discovered, go mute. They cannot justify their story.

Below, from right to left: The almshouses, the Guildhall, with schoolroom above, and the Guild Chapel, *c* 1905.

THE GUILD OF THE HOLY CROSS

As Stratford grew in prosperity and importance during the early medieval period, the townspeople began to found their own institutions. The most notable of these, the Guild of the Holy Cross, was one of a number of guilds that came into being in the early thirteenth century as a charitable body catering for the poor of the town. Its first master was Robert de Stratford, and it was given formal recognition in 1269 by Bishop Giffard, by which time it had already established an almshouse. By the end of the century it had built its chapel, on the corner of Church Street, and a Guildhall, and employed chaplains and probably a schoolmaster. Early fourteenth-century tax lists indicate that the guild was by then not only acquiring property in the town but was also performing administrative tasks on behalf of the townspeople on top of its religious and social activities.

By 1403, when it absorbed the old Guild of the Blessed Mary and St John the Baptist, it was a flourishing institution, with a wide reputation around the county and much enriched by the gifts and bequests of its members. In addition to two or more priests to say mass and pray for the souls of the departed, it consisted of a number of brothers and sisters from whose ranks were elected annually eight aldermen, a master and two proctors. These officials were responsible for the guild estate which, in 1403, included twenty messuages, three shops, a halfyard of land and some burgages in Stratford, Bridge Town and Ryon Clifford (see Glossary). After taking over the older guild, the Guild of the Holy Cross retained its hall, known as the House of St Mary, as a schoolhouse, but the master was accommodated in the 'Rood House', the Guildhall in Church Street. In 1416–17 the school followed the master to Church Street where in 1427–8 a schoolhouse with a chamber over it was built a few yards south of the chapel at a cost of a little over £10. Later in the century the Guild Chapel was enhanced by a new chancel, costing £25.

Rivalries

In the early years of the guilds' existence the priests attached to them used the altars in the north aisle at Holy Trinity to say mass. However, in the early fifteenth century, by which time the Guild of the Holy Cross had absorbed the other guilds, a dispensation was granted which allowed the guild to celebrate mass in its own Guild Chapel on the corner of what are now Church Street and Chapel Lane in the middle of town. Now there was a rival venue for mass in Stratford, and one moreover that was much more convenient for the townspeople, especially those who were old or infirm. The guild priests pressed their advantage, and timed their Sunday masses to start a little earlier than the ones at Holy Trinity. It did not take long before the priests of the guild and the priests of the college were up in arms against each other.

At stake was the supremacy of the college over the guild – not to mention the income each could hope to derive from their congregations. The bickering went on for a decade or so, until in 1432 the Pope himself was forced to intervene and issue a papal bull, in which he came down on the side of the college, ordering 'that the chaplains of the guild were not to begin masses in their chapel before the gospel at the high mass has been read in the collegiate church', which in those days was at the end of the service. That matters had reached a very low ebb is indicated by the Pope's additional stricture that this should be the case 'unless it be unduly postponed by malice in order to prevent the divine offices in their oratory'. Each side, it seems, could be as rancorous as the other.

There was more: 'They are not to stir up strife, but to make concord between the warden and his people' and 'they are not to entice the parishioners from their church, but to sustain its honour'. The churchwardens too were to be properly treated: 'Salute them with reverence, and behave to them fittingly and honestly.' The Pope's intervention seems to have had the right result; and within a century the dissolution of the guild during the reign of Edward VI removed the bone of contention entirely.

Martin Gorick: Extract from sermon series 'Between two funerals', 2006

So by 1500 the Guild Chapel, the Guildhall, the school and the almshouse formed a notable group of buildings running from the corner of Chapel Lane along Church Street, and were much as John Leland saw and admired them in 1542: 'There is a right goodly chapel in a fair street towards the south end of the town, newly re-edified by Hugh Clopton. There is a grammar school on the south side, of the foundation of one Joliffe, a Master of Art, born in Stratford. There is also an almshouse.' Today they still look much as they must have done when Leland saw them and when William Shakespeare, only a couple of decades after Leland wrote about them, might have recorded himself

> with his satchel
> And shining morning face, creeping like snail
> Unwillingly to school.
>
> (*As You Like It*, 2.7)

The fifteenth-century schoolroom above the Guildhall, still in use by King Edward VI Grammar School today.

The Guild Chapel, dedicated to the Holy Cross, was the beneficiary of much largesse from the notabilities of Stratford, including Hugh Clopton who paid for much of the building and remembered it in his will. Before the Reformation it was richly decorated, with a typical late medieval collection of narrative paintings: the martyrdom of Becket, St George and the Dragon, Solomon and the Queen of Sheba and the finding of the True Cross by St Helena, as well as the passion and death of Christ and the 'Doom', or Day of Judgement, over the chancel arch. But in 1548, the Guild fell victim to Edward VI's reforms and was dissolved, and its lands and possessions, then valued at £43 per annum, went to the Crown.

CIVIC AUTHORITY

In 1549 the townspeople of Stratford sent a petition to the king to ask for a Charter of Incorporation. Signed at Westminster on June 28 1553 – a mere eight days before Edward VI died – the charter incorporated the town and returned to it the sequestered possessions of the Guild of the Holy Cross and the college. It made provision for a bailiff, aldermen and burgesses (John Shakespeare became one of the first bailiffs) to oversee the town's affairs, a form of local government that persisted almost to the present day. The conclusion of the document read:

> ... whereupon the inhabitants have humbly besought us that we should extend our abundant grace and favour to them for the amelioration of the Borough and of the government thereof, and for the supporting of the great charges which they from time to time are forced and ought to sustain and support, and that we would deign to make, reduce and create the same inhabitants into a body Corporate and politic, know ye that we do grant that the same Borough may be a Free Borough for ever hereafter.

One of the charter's effects was to enrich the new Stratford Corporation with the wealth of the guild, which it was to use for the benefit of the town and for the relief of the poor. The royal grant included the Guild Chapel itself, which thus found itself in the unusual position of being in the ownership of the town rather than of an ecclesiastical authority.

Stratford held on to the guild's property and wealth for centuries after Edward VI gave it to them, and wise management ensured that it increased and developed, until by the end of the twentieth century there was a substantial portfolio of land, property and investments. It was then decided that it would be better placed within a charity which would administer it independently. The result was the Stratford Town Trust, which now disburses the funds and has been very generous to Holy Trinity church as well as to many other worthy local causes.

RELIGIOUS UPHEAVALS

The return to Catholicism under Edward VI's successor, Mary I, aroused strong feelings in Stratford and Warwickshire. Two Warwickshire men were among the first three to be burnt at the stake for refusing to acknowledge the new dispensation – or rather, the return to the old. In the town itself, there was a dispute between the Corporation and the queen, when in 1553 she insisted on appointing Roger Dyos, a Catholic, as vicar over the head of Edward Alcock, previously sub-warden of the college. The council refused for sixteen months to pay Dyos his stipend and then, under

The Guild Chapel exterior, above right, and interior, above, showing the remains of the pre-Reformation painting of the 'Doom', or Day of Judgement. The reconstruction, left, was done in 1954 by Wilfrid Puddephat.

pressure, gave him only ten months' worth of what he was owed, though he later sued for the remainder and won it. However, he did not long survive the return to Protestantism with the accession of Elizabeth I; he was forced by the Corporation to stand down in 1561.

Many cases of affray were presented to the Stratford courts during the high tension of these years, and it may have been at this period that many of the mutilations of Catholic imagery occurred, both in Holy Trinity church and in the Guild Chapel. It is, however, noteworthy that Stratford appears to have dragged its feet in carrying out this work; many other towns had already done so by 1560 as ordered by the new queen, whereas Stratford took two or three years more to decide to obey.

Whether or not the covering of the images was done reluctantly, it became evident in 1804, when the Doom fresco in the Guild Chapel was rediscovered from under the whitewash in fairly good condition, that some of the paintings had been attacked with sharp instruments. In any event, the chapel in the early 1560s was now fit to follow the new ordinance: as a whitewashed auditorium for the preaching of the Word of God, it had replaced the superstitious objects of veneration with a suitable environment for the transmission and understanding of true doctrine.

The chapel today has changed again: still owned by the town rather than by the church, it is now a non-denominational place of worship, a chapel of unity where priests of Holy Trinity hold a Eucharist every week with other more occasional ecumenical services. It also remains – as it always has been – the building used for worship by the staff and boys of King Edward VI Grammar School. And it is still the home of the curfew bell, originally cast and hung there in 1633, which rings out at 8pm every day.

KING EDWARD VI GRAMMAR SCHOOL

Ronnie Mulryne

1553 was a crucial year for both Holy Trinity church and the Grammar School. The school could already trace a long history, stretching back to the appointment of a schoolmaster shortly after the foundation of the Guild of the Holy Cross in 1269, and had been enhanced by Thomas Jolyffe's endowment in 1482. The church could look back on a history that was even longer. But the events of the Reformation and the adjustments to patterns of worship and civic organisation that followed profoundly affected both church and education – the essential building blocks of local as well as national society. The college of priests was dissolved in 1547 and the Guild of the Holy Cross, with its altars in Holy Trinity and its patronage of education and what we now call the social services (the almshouses, for example, and care for the bereaved), was brought to an end at the same time. A new civic order was needed, and this was made possible in the dying weeks of Edward VI's life by the provision of the new Town Charter.

Among the charter's provisions was the requirement that a 'Free Grammar School for the instruction and education of the boys and youths there shall be hereafter kept up and maintained as heretofore hath been used'. And it made financial provision out of the revenues of the former college and guild to pay both the schoolmaster and the vicar the relatively handsome sum of £20 each per annum, and to provide each of them with a 'convenient dwelling house or mansion within the said town of Stratford-upon-Avon'. The guild and college estates, set up at this time, remained in existence until 2001 when they were incorporated into the newly formed Town Trust. The charter also provided for 'a chaplain being a priest in the said parish church of Stratford-upon-Avon yearly for ever to serve and to assist the said vicar', bestowing on him 'ten pounds of lawful money' per annum.

There is no direct evidence that William Shakespeare attended the Grammar School; but his status as the son of a burgess would have entitled him to do so, and the breadth of knowledge displayed in his works is proof enough that he was a well educated man. He almost certainly learned to read and write in the Guild Chapel, where the 'petty school' was held, supervised by the 'usher', the schoolmaster's assistant; and from there he would have gone on to the Grammar School, and been taught in the room above the Guildhall which is still part of the school today and still much as he would have known it.

School and church have been closely associated almost throughout their history, with vicars and assistant priests regularly serving as schoolmasters, with the early history of the school being tied in with the Guild of the Holy Cross and the parish church – there is a possibility that in the early days classes were held in the church – and with, in more recent times, sidespeople, churchwardens and directors of music being drawn from teachers and governors of the school. The education, baptism and burial of the great dramatist are therefore shared between the two institutions – a connection that is today honoured both in the annual Shakespeare procession led by the school, in benefactors' and carol services and in the series of 'Playing with History' pageants that the boys have regularly performed in the church building.

A nineteenth-century watercolour of the school courtyard.

THE STRATFORD CHURCH COURT – THE 'BAWDY COURT'

A regular monthly date in the calendar of the Holy Trinity authorities was the convening of the church court, commonly known as the 'bawdy court' – though one Thomas Faux, who lived in Stratford during Shakespeare's lifetime, was hauled up before it on a charge of 'scandalising this court' by using that name for it. He was certainly not alone in using the expression; although the church courts dealt with many religious crimes, a large number of them related to matters sexual, hence the colloquial term.

In today's more secular world, it is easy to forget that in the medieval and immediately post-medieval world both church and state ruled the lives of the citizens, and everyone was subject to both religious and secular laws. Church courts met regularly to consider reports on their parishes tendered by the churchwardens, and to summon those who were accused of 'adultery, whoredom, incest, drunkenness, swearing, ribaldry, usury, absence from church on Sundays or holy days, disorderly behaviour in church, blasphemy, scandal-mongering, bigamy, irregular marriage, not contributing to the church rate…' – in other words, any of a number of social, sexual and religious misdemeanours.

In Stratford, Holy Trinity church was the venue for the church court, presided over by the vicar who sat in judgement there about once a month. It is not known for sure where the court convened, but it is likely to have been either the parvise or muniments room above the north porch or the north-west corner of the nave, where the shop now is. A few records for the Holy Trinity court survive (now deposited in the Kent Archive Office in Maidstone among the Sackville of Knole Manuscripts), among them two Act Books which include mentions of members of Shakespeare's family and also throw a great deal of light on the lives of other townspeople of Stratford at the time. One of these

For the rebellion of a codpiece to take away the life of a man!

(*MEASURE FOR MEASURE*, 3.1)

starts in 1590 and goes on until 1616 but with large gaps; the other is a pretty comprehensive record for the years 1622–4.

The penalties available to the Church Court were local and social rather than penal. They could levy fines, but could not send the guilty to the gallows or to prison, though persistent offenders could be handed over to the secular authorities for more severe punishment. But in that much smaller and more enclosed world, where everyone knew everyone else, they had a much more potent weapon at their disposal: public shame.

A man or woman hauled up before the court to answer a charge brought by an accuser might admit guilt and repent of the crime, in which case he or she would be warned against future sins or, if the matter was regarded as serious, ordered to do penance. This involved standing up in church on a Sunday, in full view of the congregation of family, friends and neighbours, and confessing the sin in detail – a heavy blow to the penitent's reputation and credit, particularly for those high up in the social scale where public repute was all-important. For major crimes, this public confession acquired an added shame: it had to be performed bareheaded and barefoot while wearing a white sheet and carrying a white rod – a 'white sheet penance', signifying both a dreadful sin and deep repentance. Sometimes the penance had to be done more than once on consecutive Sundays, and in the worst cases also in the town on market day. For those who could afford it, however, an alternative could usually be negotiated – the payment of a hefty fine which would be used for the benefit of the poor of the parish and a private penance before a priest.

Those who denied the charge had to 'purge' themselves, either on their own account or with the support of witnesses, and the court would take a view on guilt or innocence. But for anyone failing to answer the summons to appear before the court, and thus considered 'contumacious', the penalty was excommunication. This again was a heavy price to pay: being cut off from the church was in effect exclusion from society; and for major offenders, who were sentenced to a more severe form of excommunication, this could mean

The Shakespeare family and the Holy Trinity 'bawdy court'

There is no record that William Shakespeare was ever summoned to appear before the church court, but it is possible that his having got his wife pregnant before they married would have had this consequence. The marriage laws were still unclear in the late sixteenth century, and the custom whereby 'spousals', or a binding promise to marry, allowed the forthcoming marriage to be consummated was increasingly being called into question by more puritan clergy. The Stratford records show that between 1570 and 1630 only three men in the town married before the age of twenty (Shakespeare was unusually young, being only eighteen, and the average age was twenty-four), and of those three he was the only one whose wife was already pregnant. The new Mr and Mrs Shakespeare may well, like others who do appear in the records, have been called to account for their premature enjoyment of the marriage bed; but there is no evidence.

However, the Act Books which sporadically cover the years 1590 to 1624 include several references to Shakespeare's family. On the side of the law were Anne Shakespeare's brother, Bartholomew Hathaway, and his son and grandson, who all appear in the records as churchwardens and executors. On the other side were members of the poet's own family who were summoned to answer accusations.

Both brother Richard and sister Joan (Hart) appeared before the court on separate occasions in 1608, but the record does not detail what the charges were or, in Joan's case, the penalty. Richard was fined a shilling for the poor of the parish.

Shakespeare's daughter Susanna was one of those caught up in the campaign of 1606 against those not fulfilling their religious obligations. She failed initially to turn up to answer the charge, and the matter was postponed to the next occasion, when a clerk's note of dismissal in the margin leads to the assumption that she had made a promise to conform in future.

> *Poor soul, the centre of my*
> *sinful earth.*
>
> (SONNET 146)

Then in 1613, when she was aged thirty and married to John Hall, she was the subject of a slanderous accusation by one John Lane, who claimed that she 'had the running of the reins and had been naught[y] with Ralph Smith at John Palmer's', ie that she had caught a venereal disease after having illicit sexual intercourse with Smith, a hatter and haberdasher. This case was regarded as serious enough to be taken to the Consistory Court at Worcester, where her name was cleared after Lane failed to attend the court; he was excommunicated.

Considerably more damaging to the Shakespeare family was the case of Thomas Quiney, who became Shakespeare's son-in-law when he married Judith Shakespeare on February 10 1616. Before and around the time of the wedding there was a persistent rumour that Quiney had made Margaret Wheeler pregnant. In the middle of March, only weeks after the wedding, both she and the baby died in childbirth and were buried in Holy Trinity.

Thomas Quiney was hauled up before the court on March 26 where he confessed to the crime and was sentenced to a severe punishment: a full white sheet penance in the church on three consecutive Sundays. He offered five shillings instead, which was accepted; but he still had to acknowledge his fault in front of a minister, though he was allowed to do this while dressed normally and in private in the chapel at Bishopton. This disgrace to the family almost certainly caused his father-in-law to change his will, in which he now gave Judith a legacy in her own name, and can have done little to ease his last days; he was buried on April 25, only a few weeks after these events.

being cut off totally from the protection of the state and the law, a situation that could only be relieved by absolution and the payment of a large fine.

During the years for which we have records, there were three main categories of crime brought before the Holy Trinity 'bawdy court': failure to adhere to the requirements of religious practice; disorderly behaviour; and sexual misdemeanours.

The first of these usually involved non-attendance at church on Sundays and feast days, and in particular failure to receive Holy Communion at least three times a year, including at Easter. Those who did not obey these rules were usually suspected of being 'church papists' – Catholics or people with strong Catholic sympathies. After the Gunpowder Plot of 1605, when the crackdown on Catholicism intensified, the rules and penalties became considerably more severe, with a fine of £20 imposed on those who failed to obey in the first year, rising to £40 in year two and £60 in year three – huge sums of money then.

The Stratford records reflect this new stringency. In May 1606, as part of what was clearly a campaign, twenty-one townspeople appeared before the court accused of failing to

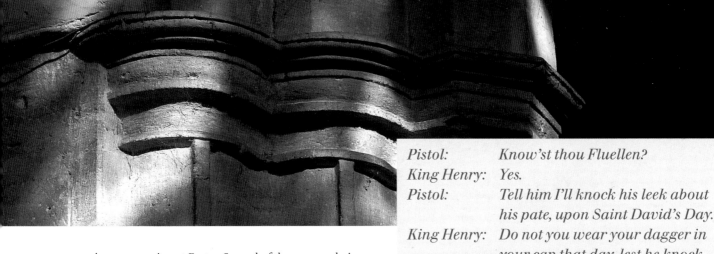

Pistol:	*Know'st thou Fluellen?*
King Henry:	*Yes.*
Pistol:	*Tell him I'll knock his leek about his pate, upon Saint David's Day.*
King Henry:	*Do not you wear your dagger in your cap that day, lest he knock that about yours.*

(HENRY V, 4.1)

receive communion at Easter. Several of them were obvious Catholic sympathisers. Margaret Reynolds had already paid a monthly fine for recusancy, and was known to have given refuge two years previously to a fugitive Jesuit priest. Hamnet Sadler was also among those accused. He and his wife Judith were the godparents of Hamnet and Judith Shakespeare, and on this occasion 'petitioned for time to clear his conscience'.

Several of the Holy Trinity vicars at this time were strong Sabbatarians, members of a Puritan wing of the church who came down hard on desecration of the Sabbath. John Bramhall, who arrived in 1589, attributed the great fires of 1594 and 1595, both of which he alleged had broken out on a Sunday, to God's wrath against townspeople who had failed to observe the Sabbath day properly. He used the church court energetically as a means of ensuring that those who profaned the Sabbath were named, shamed and punished. The churchwardens and town constable were enjoined to check who were 'in any alehouses or inns or other suspected places in gaming or tippling, or otherwise' during the times of divine service, and they were also to 'diligently view and see what persons do use to bowl or play at any games at times aforesaid'. In October 1592 no fewer than thirty-seven people were accused of opening their shops on Sundays or holy days, as compared with seven accusations of fornication, one of keeping evil company and one of slander. One Joan Tawnte admitted 'going out of the church with beckoning with her finger and laughing, also for swearing by the name of God'. She was sentenced to public penance, but was at least allowed to perform it in her own clothes.

One William Llewellyn (spelt Flewellyn in the Act Book; cf Fluellen in *Henry V*) was indicted in 1590 for opening his shop on the Sabbath, as was Shakespeare's godfather William Smith, a haberdasher.

Some of those accused were persistent in their defiance: one Ralph Lorde was particularly incorrigible, being accused on the first occasion of having 'encouraged in his house in time of divine service certain persons eating and drinking', and then later 'for the misuse of Sunday in the selling of meat in the time of divine service' and later again 'for drinking on the Sabbath day in prayer time'. And the clash of a major religious feast day with a secular holiday could lead to a summons. John Allen was sentenced to do penance for 'dancing the morris' in evening prayer time on May Day, which also happened to be the feast of St Philip and St James.

The church court clearly had some hard cases to contend with. Stephen Lea was arraigned 'for singing profane and filthy songs, scoffing and deriding of ministers and the profession of religion'. And Elizabeth Wheeler, when had up for brawling, turned on the vicar with the words 'God's wounds, a plague a God on you all, a fart of one's arse for you'. He was outraged, and excommunicated her.

Yet it seemed that the church could condemn reprehensible behaviour on the one hand while, on the other, entrusting its perpetrator with responsibility. Augustine Boyce was employed by the parish to take care of the fabric of the church and to supervise the scholars during services; yet he also appeared before the court twice, in 1628 and in 1633. On the first occasion he had stolen the communion wine; on the second, he was accused of 'tippling and suffering the bell ringers to tipple and drink at the communion table in the chancel and for slobbering and fouling the same'.

Sexual crimes usually attracted white sheet penance, often on more than one Sunday and on market day too. This was the punishment meted out to John Sadler in May 1606 after Anne Browne confessed that she was pregnant by him. He failed to respond to the first summons, and suffered the indignity of finding the second citation nailed to his door. The outcome for him is not known, since the record is silent; but the baptismal register for June 7 1606 is clear enough: 'Katheryn, daughter to Anne Browne als Watton, notha [illegitimate]'.

GOOD FREND FOR IE

TO DIGG THE DVS

BLESE BE YE MAN

AND CVRST BE HE

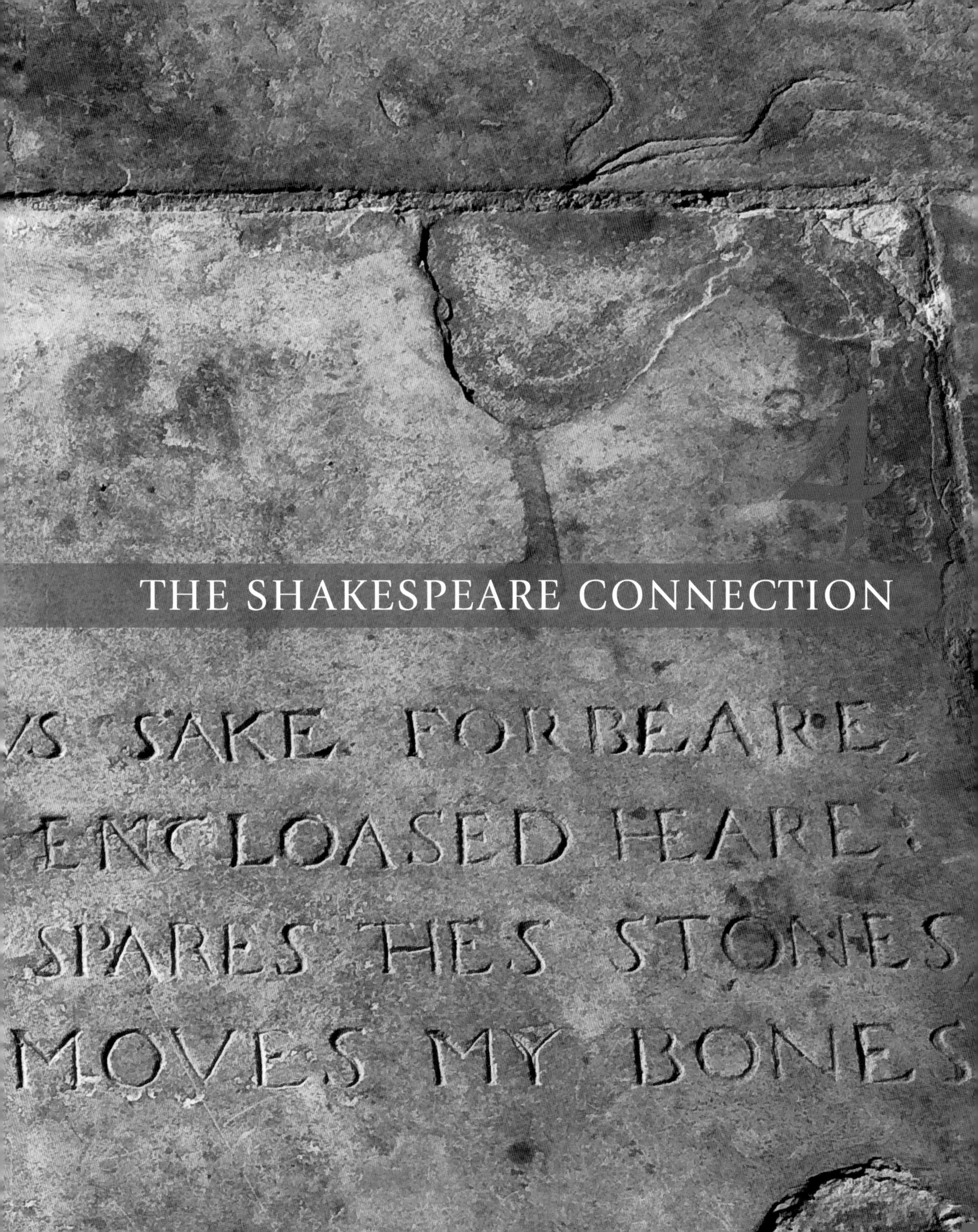
VS SAKE FORBEARE,
ENCLOASED HEARE:
SPARES THES STONES
MOVES MY BONES

4 THE SHAKESPEARE CONNECTION

Let's talk of graves, of worms, of epitaphs.

(RICHARD II, 3. 2)

THE CHURCH AS PART OF SHAKESPEARE'S LIFE

The first mention of William Shakespeare in the annals of Holy Trinity church is the record of his baptism in the parish register for April 26 1564: 'Gulielmus filius Johannes Shakspeare'; 'William, son of John Shakespeare'. By the time of his burial, on April 25 1616, the parish records were being written in English, not Latin; his read merely 'Will Shakspeare, Gent'.

Thus did Holy Trinity mark the beginning and end of his life. The church records, however, make no mention of the other major religious ceremony which he celebrated, his marriage to Anne Hathaway. No parish records survive to confirm or deny the claims to the event made by various local churches.

Stratford's parish church would, however, have played a major part in the life of the young man who grew up in the town, who went to school there and whose family were prominent residents. The damaged font that now sits in the chancel was the one in which he was baptised, and where he saw his children baptised. He would have stood in the porch with his daughters at their weddings, ready to lead them up the aisle. On his way into the chancel he would have passed through the door in the original rood screen – the one that now shuts off the north transept from the crossing – and his body was carried through that door for burial in his grave in the chancel itself. Members of his family – his wife, his daughter, his son-in-law and his granddaughter's first husband – are buried beside him in the chancel, and other family

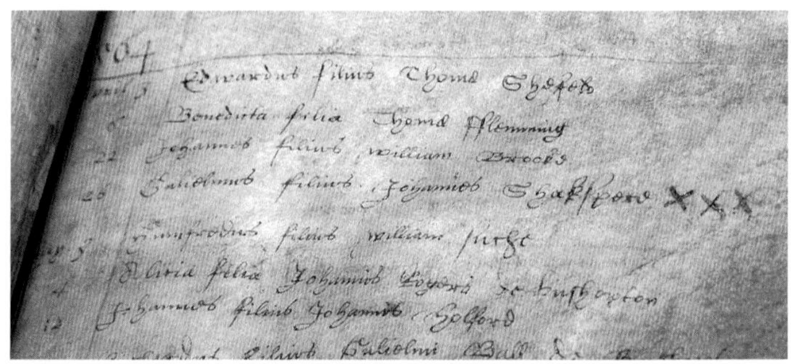

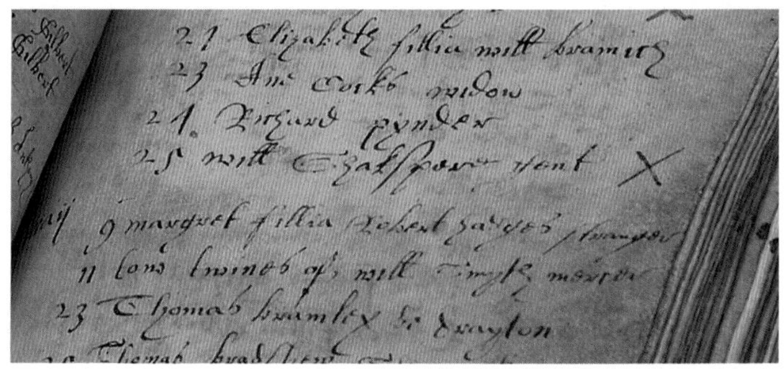

Above left: A corner of the register.

Above: The registrations of Shakespeare's baptism and burial held in The Shakespeare Birthplace Trust; those displayed in the church are copies.

Opposite: The closing ring, or sanctuary knocker, on the inner door of the north porch.

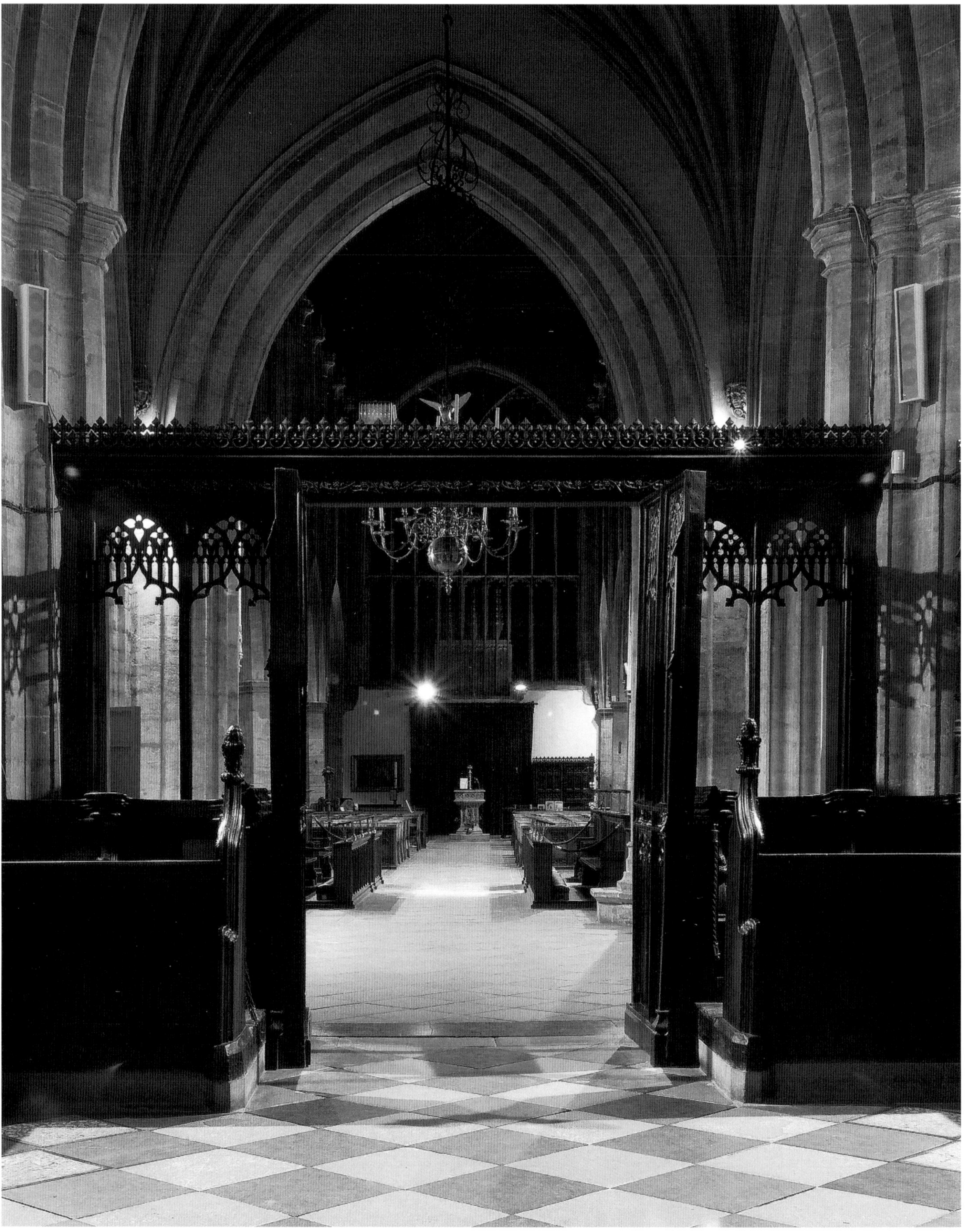

Shakespeare's ring?

The story of this ring, now on display at The Shakespeare Birthplace Trust, was told by Robert Bell Wheler, the Stratford historian. In 1810 a labourer's wife found a signet ring in a field next to the churchyard; oddly, a man called William Shakespeare was working in the field at the time. Wheler bought it for the price of its weight in gold on the day it was found, by which time it had already been immersed in 'aquafortis' to remove the encrustations. The ring is engraved with the letters W S with a lover's knot in between. Wheler wrote that in spite of 'numerous researches into public and private documents' he could find 'no Stratfordian of that period so likely to own such a ring as Shakespeare'.

It is more than possible that this rather splendid ring was indeed the property of William Shakespeare: it is of the right period, and he would certainly have owned such a thing. The conjecture is given added weight by the fact that in the amended version of his will, which was signed just before his death, in the line 'whereof I have hereunto put my Seale' the word 'Seale' is crossed out and replaced by 'hand'.

Michael Wood, in *In Search of Shakespeare*, allows himself to imagine that on a cold day in February, while attending his daughter Judith's wedding, her father may have taken off his gloves to shake hands with a friend after the ceremony and failed to notice that his ring had fallen off. He was within weeks of his death, and so may have lost weight through illness, hence the ring being loose. It is plausible.

I have lost a seal-ring of my grandfather's worth forty mark.

(HENRY IV PART 1, 3.3)

Opposite: The nave from the chancel.

members in the churchyard: his father and mother, his sister and two of his brothers, his son Hamnet, who was buried there aged eleven in August 1596, and his daughter Judith, though she greatly outlived the rest of family and did not die until 1662 when she was seventy-seven years old. Judith lost all three of her sons in her own lifetime: the first-born, named Shakespeare, in infancy, and the other two, Richard and Thomas, aged twenty-one and nineteen, in the same month of January 1639, presumably of plague. They too probably lie under the Holy Trinity turf, as does her husband Thomas Quiney, though his date of death is unknown. The only granddaughter William actually knew, Elizabeth, married again after Thomas Nash died and is buried elsewhere.

William Shakespeare would, like everyone else in Stratford, have been summoned by the bells to services, taken his due part in them in the nave and joined in all the other activities of the town which centred on the church. The Holy Trinity church that he knew was, however, very different from the one we see now – and also very different from the one with which his parents had grown up. John and Mary Shakespeare and their contemporaries had to deal with unsettling upheavals in religious beliefs and practices, and had to learn to adapt to new ways which had moved radically away from the old. Their son grew up under the new ordinance, and knew nothing other than a church where all the so-called idolatrous images had been destroyed or covered over and where the forms of worship that his parents had known were long gone.

It is possible, however, that the new practices which Shakespeare followed may in later life have given him, as a prominent and educated citizen of the town, a closer involvement with worship in the church. Under the Catholic ordinance the celebrant was a remote figure, far away in the chancel which itself was closed off by the rood screen, conducting the service with his back to the congregation and speaking in Latin. Worshippers could see and hear what was going on, but they were at the same time separate from it, both physically and liturgically. The mystery was for the priest alone; those present were part of it but at a distance.

By contrast, the new Protestant ordinance, which developed and changed still further as Puritanism and Sabbatarianism grew stronger towards the end of the sixteenth century, embraced the ideal of 'the priesthood of all the faithful' and the link between celebrant and congregation grew closer. Might it therefore be plausible to conjecture that members of the congregation were called on as lay readers to play a part in the services, perhaps by reading the lesson from the Bible? Is it possible that William Shakespeare himself was called on to read from the chained Bible, the first edition of the King James Bible dating to 1611, that was there in his time and is still in the church today? It was certainly within Holy Trinity that he first heard the words of the Bible and Prayer Book that were to have such a strong influence on his work. It is a beguiling thought that it was in this very book that he read those words.

There were, however, some elements of the church William Shakespeare knew which had been there in his parents' youth; nor have later changes swept away everything with which he would have been in his turn familiar. As a young man he would certainly have enjoyed the carvings on the misericord seats, and the masks that today hang on the old rood screen would have been among the adornments of the chancel roof. Like visitors today, he might have wondered at the mutilations to the images of God and Christ on Balsall's tomb and elsewhere in the building; but other elements of the rich medieval carving were still there to be seen and relished. And his hand certainly touched the ancient knocker on the inner porch doors.

Shakespeare and Psalm 46

The Holy Trinity Bible is usually open at Psalm 46, which has an intriguing connection with Shakespeare. In the first four months of 1611, when this first edition of the new King James Bible was published, Shakespeare was aged forty-six; he turned forty-seven in April that year. Ignoring the title of the psalm, if you count down to the forty-sixth word you will find 'shake'. If you then go the end of the psalm, ignore the word 'selah', which is like 'amen', and count forty-six words back, you will find the word 'spear'.

There is no evidence at all that Shakespeare was involved with the translation of the King James Bible, which must anyway have been going on for several years and can't have been reliably expected to be ready to reach publication during part of the poet's forty-sixth year. The idea that he worked his name into the psalm is fanciful; but it demonstrates the intrigue which inevitably clusters around him.

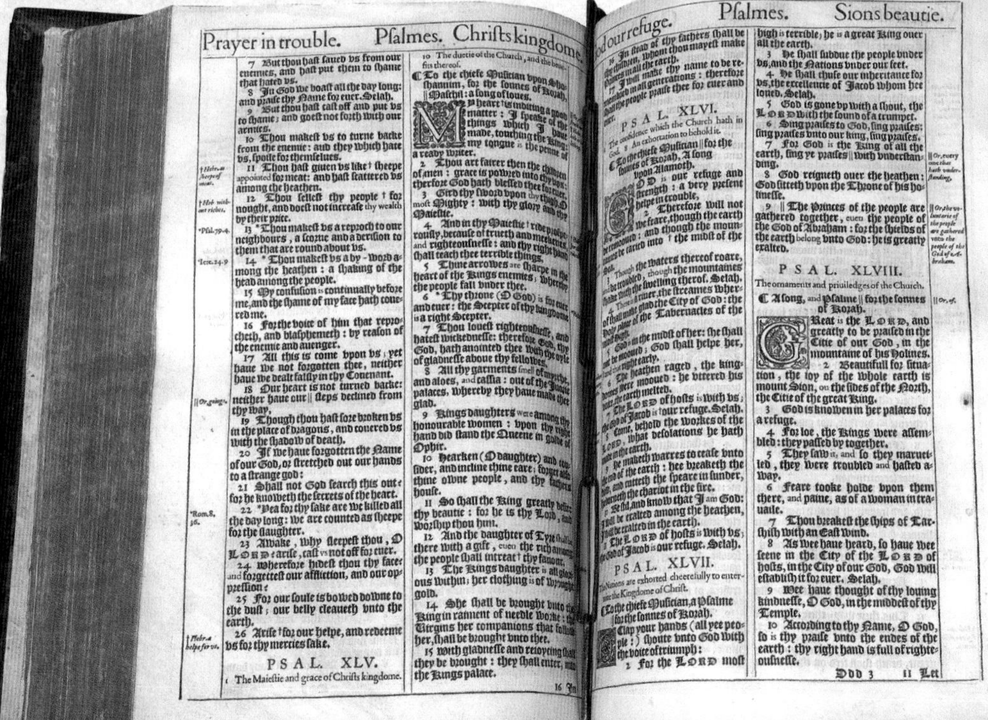

Holy Trinity's King James Bible, a first edition from 1611.

Shakespeare and spirituality

In exploring Shakespeare's spirituality, we need to engage with the scope of his imagination and ask ourselves how that might be revealing of a sense of faith in God, how Shakespeare's 'visible' *work* makes present a sense of the 'invisible' *world*.

At his most metaphysical, Shakespeare articulates universal doubts. In *All's Well That Ends Well* (2.3.4–6), the Lord Lafeu warns us against making 'trifles of terrors, ensconcing ourselves into seeming knowledge when we should submit ourselves to an unknown fear', that is fear of the unknown. Antonio in *The Tempest* (2.1.282–3) articulates crisply the voice of a non-believer: 'I feel not/This deity in my bosom'. *King Lear* explores humanity's own sense of relationship to 'the gods' more than any other play. When Lear enters carrying his dead daughter Cordelia we hear:

> Howl, howl, howl, howl! O, you are men of
> stones.
> Had I your tongues and eyes, I'd use them so
> That heaven's vault should crack.
>
> (*The Tragedy of King Lear*, 5.3.232–4)

Shakespeare is here depicting a profound sense of relationship with the divine, albeit one grounded in anger and despair. A few moments later Lear, considering his daughter's corpse, asks one of the most straightforward questions about the purpose of human existence in the whole of English literature:

> No, no, no life?
> Why should a dog, a horse, a rat have life,
> And thou no breath at all?
>
> (*The Tragedy of King Lear*, 5.3.281–3)

Shakespeare alludes to the Bible many hundreds of times (there were no fewer than 350 reprints of the Bible in English between 1525 and his death in 1616), and draws readily on Christian themes. In Sonnet 146 (lines 13–14) he hints at a resurrection by imagining the soul feeding on death

> that feeds on men,
> And death once dead, there's no more dying
> then.

Major resurrection narratives can be found in numerous plays, when characters who have been supposed dead come back to life: twin masters and servants as well as the Abbess in *The Comedy of Errors*, Hero in *Much Ado About Nothing*, the twins Viola and Sebastian in *Twelfth Night, or what you will*, Claudio in *Measure for Measure*, Thaisa in *Pericles*, Posthumus in *Cymbeline* and, perhaps most miraculously of all, Queen Hermione in *The Winter's Tale*.

Shakespeare, 'with whom', as his monument on the north wall of the chancel in Holy Trinity church tells us, 'quick nature died', also expresses a spirituality through the natural world. Often this leads to arrestingly precise details. When, in *Cymbeline*, Imogen awakes to find what she supposes is the headless corpse of her husband alongside her, she makes the following prayer:

> Good faith,
> I tremble still with fear; but if there be
> Yet left in heaven as small a drop of pity
> As a wren's eye, feared gods, a part of it!
>
> (*Cymbeline*, 4.2.304–7)

To find the infinite and the divine in something as small and specific as a 'wren's eye' suggests a spirituality rooted in the Christian belief in the incarnation, of God becoming flesh and interacting with God's world, drawing everything to God through the person of Jesus.

Just before Hamlet's fateful duel with Laertes, Horatio offers to send word that Hamlet is not fit to fight, and Hamlet replies:

> Not a whit. We defy augury. There is special providence in the fall of a sparrow. If it be now, 'tis not to come. If it be not to come, it will be now. If it be not now, yet it will come. The readiness is all. Since no man knows aught of what he leaves, what is't to leave betimes? Let be.
>
> (*Hamlet* 5.2.213–18, quoted from *The Penguin Shakespeare*)

Here, Shakespeare's reference to the natural world deliberately coincides with Matthew's gospel (10:28–31) to convey Hamlet's feelings. There is acceptance and resignation in the shape and structure of Hamlet's language, as well as a quiet, confident and calm affirmation of a universal truth and question: how ready will any of us be to die when the time comes? From a spiritual perspective, Hamlet's speech is as good an articulation of grace – of a dependency on God – as you can find anywhere in Shakespeare.

It is the poet's privilege to imagine the world differently, to enhance lives through the use of language, to help us to identify our own experiences and feelings, as well as to take us to other worlds. Looking for spirituality in Shakespeare reveals a writer equally able to articulate grace and despair, one who expresses a faith rooted in the particularity of human experience and the natural world, and who is not afraid to ask the searching questions that trouble us all.

Paul Edmondson

Come, boy; I am past more children, but thy sons and daughters will be all gentlemen born.

(*THE WINTER'S TALE*, 5.2)

Opposite: Detail of Shakespeare's monument on the north wall of the chancel.

THE MONUMENT AND THE GRAVE

Shakespeare's burial entry in the parish register reads merely, 'Will Shakespeare, Gent'. That he was a local citizen of substance is undoubted; that he was also a 'gentleman' is clear, since he had inherited the arms granted to his father: 'Or, on a bend sable, a tilting spear of the first, point upwards headed argent. Crest, a falcon displayed argent, supporting a spear in pale or' (see Glossary for the meaning). His fame as a poet and playwright was certainly well established at the time of his death.

However, it is unlikely that it was his artistic reputation that earned him his prominent burial place in the chancel of Holy Trinity. Nor is it likely that it arose from his possibly being a lay rector, as is sometimes claimed from his tenancy of a lease on a half share of the tithes due to the church, purchased in 1605 for £440. Tithe tenancy committed him to contribute towards the upkeep of the chancel; but it did not carry an automatic right to burial there. And apart from clear evidence that many non-tithe tenants – including several members of the Shakespeare family – were buried in the chancel, the Corporation's dispute in 1618 with the vicar, John Rogers, shows that the issue ultimately came down to payment. Local historian Robert Bearman, working from unpublished orders of the Stratford Corporation, believes that:

> burial in the chancel was a separate issue, requiring the payment of fees, and could be a useful source of income: but clearly there was scope for a quarrel here, between the vicar and the tithe owners… On December 4 1618, two years after Shakespeare's burial, the Corporation, as owners of the tithes, passed a resolution: 'that the chamberlains shall discharge Mr Rogers [the vicar] from receiving any more benefit by burials in the chancel, that the chamberlains shall receive it henceforth towards the repair of the chancel… and also to demand of Mr Rogers so much as he hath received within this last year'. Clearly the Corporation took the view, as ultimate tithe owners, that if fees were paid for burial in the chancel, then those fees should go towards the repair of the chancel: the vicar must have been seeing things differently, regarding such fees as his own. But it is clear that anybody could be buried in the chancel if the family could pay for the privilege, either to the vicar or the Corporation. Indeed, some asked to be buried in the chancel in their wills – Margaret Reynolds, for instance, in May 1615; whereas John Smith, in 1613, specified the south aisle, and Robert Salisbury the middle aisle, near his pew. Some just said vaguely in the church or churchyard. Shakespeare, somewhat unusually and perhaps interestingly, is even more vague ('my body to the earth') and so it was family, and maybe friends, who must have decided to do the honours.

Such high status last resting places were therefore reserved for those who could pay for them; as is shown by the 1836 plan (page 81), the chancel floor was in fact a sea of graves, which are still there under the flagstones. Burial there was prestigious, but by no means exclusive.

There is a tradition that Shakespeare was buried seventeen feet deep, as an added disincentive, on top of the 'curse' inscribed on his gravestone, to those who might later be inclined to dig him up. This is highly unlikely, both because of the proximity of the river, and the consequent high water table, and because excavating such a deep grave would have been a major undertaking at that time, even more so since it would have had to be carried out within the walls of a building that was in daily use.

That the gravestone and the monument were in place in the church very soon after Shakespeare's death we know from Thomas Digges' lines in the First Folio, published seven years later in 1623:

> Shakespeare, at length thy pious fellows give
> The world thy Workes; thy workes, by which outlive
> Thy Tombe, thy name must; when that stone is rent,
> And Time dissolves thy Stratford Moniment
> Here we alive shall view thee still.

The same sentiment – that Shakespeare's works are his true monument – is expressed in the epitaph written for him by

altar
IVDICIO PYLIVM, GENIO SOCRATEM, ARTE MARONEM,
TERRA TEGIT, POPVLVS MÆRET, OLYMPVS HABE

Left and opposite: Shakespeare's monument and a detail of the hands.
Below: The inscription at the base of the monument.

I'll break my staff,
Bury it certain fathoms in the earth,
And deeper than did ever plummet sound
I'll drown my book.

(*THE TEMPEST*, 5.1)

his near-contemporary, the young John Milton, published in 1632 in the Second Folio:

> What needs my Shakespeare for his honoured bones
> The labour of an age in piled stones?
> Or that his hallowed relics should be hid
> Under a star-ypointing pyramid?
> Dear son of memory, great heir of fame,
> What need'st thou such weak witness of thy name?
> Thou in our wonder and astonishment
> Has built thyself a livelong monument.
> For whilst, to the shame of slow-endeavouring art,
> Thy easy numbers flow, and that each heart
> Hath from the leaves of thy unvalued book
> Those Delphic lines with deep impression took;
> Then thou, our fancy of itself bereaving,
> Dost make us marble with too much conceiving,
> And so sepulchred in such pomp dost lie
> That kings for such a tomb would wish to die.

Shakespeare himself left no provision in his will for any monument, and we can only presume, in the absence of any evidence as to who paid for it, that it must, as Robert Bearman suggests, have been family and perhaps friends. Germaine Greer, in her book *Shakespeare's Wife*, suggests that his widow may have been responsible (and, indeed, that she may have had a hand in the publication of the First Folio), though it is more likely that the funds were found by his daughter, Susanna Hall, and her husband John, who were the major beneficiaries of Shakespeare's will.

The monument

Shakespeare's monument is placed above head height on the north wall of the chancel, between Thomas Balsall's tomb and the door which once led to the old charnel house. The waist-length portrait bust sits in a niche with an entablature above supported on black marble columns with acanthus leaf capitals. Above are the arms granted to the Shakespeare family in the late 1590s, supported by a cherub on either side, one holding an inverted torch and the other a spade. The whole is topped by a skull.

The figure portrays a slightly chubby-faced, balding man whose hands rest on a tasselled cushion; one of them holds a pen, the other rests on a piece of paper. Said to have been the work of Gheerart Janssen, whose workshop was in Southwark

IVDICIO PYLIVM, GENIO SOCRATEM, ARTE MARON
TERRA TEGIT, POPVLVS MÆRET, OLYMPVS H
STAY PASSENGER, WHY GOEST THOV BY SO FAS
READ IF THOV CANST, WHOM ENVIOVS DEATH HATH PLA
WITH IN THIS MONVMENT SHAKSPEARE: WITH WHOM
QVICK NATVRE DIDE WHOSE NAME, DOTH DECK Y^S TOMB
FAR MORE, THEN COST: SIEH ALL, Y^T HE HATH WRITT
LEAVES LIVING ART, BVT PAGE, TO SERVE HIS WIT
OBIIT ANO DO 161
ÆTATIS 53 DIE 2

near the Globe Theatre, its early placing in the church, during the lifetime of his widow and daughters, indicates that it must be a faithful likeness. It certainly bears a close resemblance to the equally early engraving by Martin Droeshout in the First Folio.

The inscription below reads:

> *Judicio Pylium, Genio Socratem, Arte Maronem*
> *Terra tegit, populus maeret, Olympus habet.*
> Stay passenger, why goest thou by so fast,
> Read, if thou canst, whom envious death hath plast
> Within this monument: Shakespeare, with whome
> Quick nature dide whose name doth deck ys tomb,
> Far more than cost: sieth all yt he hath writt
> Leaves living art, but page, to serve his witt
> *Obiit Ano Doi 1616*
> *Aetatis 53 Die 23 Ap*

The top two lines in Latin translate as 'Earth covers, the nation mourns, and heaven holds/a Nestor in counsel, a Socrates in mind, a Virgil in art' (see Glossary).

As with the grave itself (see page 119), questions have been raised over the years about the authenticity of the monument, with those doubting it tending to suggest that it originally showed its subject not as a writer but as a 'sackholder' or a dealer in commodities, and that the cushion on which the hands rest is a woolsack. The basis for this claim is Wenceslaus Hollar's engraving of the monument, which was first published in Dugdale's *Warwickshire* in 1656. That engraving differs so radically from the current monument that it spawned the theory that the original portrait bust, assumed to have been faithfully reproduced by Hollar, had been replaced in 1749 when renovations to it took place, and that it was then that the image was doctored to show a man of letters rather than one of business.

In an article entitled 'Reconsidering Shakespeare's monument', published in 1997 in the *Review of English Studies*, Diana Price sets out the story of the doubts about the monument's authenticity, and argues convincingly that the original on which Hollar based his engraving was flawed. It has been acknowledged for some time that Hollar worked not from the monument itself but from the drawing of it made *c* 1634 by William Dugdale himself and still in the possession of the Dugdale family. As Ms Price shows, that drawing – the earliest known of the monument – is a mere sketch which appears to have been hastily drawn initially in pencil and inked in later; and though it differs in some

In the North wall of the Chancell
is this Monument fixt.
Iudicio Pylium, genio Socratem, arte Maronem
Terra tegit, populus maret, olympus habet,
Stay passenger why goest thou by soe fast,
Read, if thou canst whom envious death hath plac't
wth in this monument Shakspeare with whome
Quick nature dyed, whose name doth deck the tombe
Far more then cost, sith all that he hath writ
Leaues living art but page to serue his witt.
Obijt A.Dni. 1616
æt. 53, die 23 Apri:
Neare the wall where this monument is erected
lyeth a plaine free stone, underneath wch his
body is buried, wth this Epitaph,
Good freind for Iesus sake forbeare
To digg the dust enclosed here
Blest be the man that spares these stones
And curst be he that moves my bones

Sir William Dugdale's sketch of Shakespeare's monument, made *c* 1634.

details from the monument as we know it, in other ways it corresponds to it. It was not, therefore, a careful drawing, and was not sufficiently detailed to have supplied Hollar with enough specifics to allow him to produce an accurate rendition of the monument.

Crucial to the doubters is that the sketch shows no quill and no paper. Yet the absence of the quill is unsurprising. It was an easily removable souvenir, and is also absent in later representations of the monument. And the paper may simply have been missed by Dugdale, who was drawing the monument nearly twenty years after it was made, in an ill-lit chancel where the smoke from candles may have already spread a layer of grime over it. Dugdale also shows the cushion as much larger and lumpier than in its current form, and Hollar's engraving goes even further, representing it as much more like a woolsack, with bunches at the corners rather than tassels. Again, this anomaly can plausibly be ascribed to the sketchiness of Dugdale's effort. Although he was well known for his desire for accuracy, he did not claim to be any sort of artist. After all, over the page is his equally badly drawn illustration of the Clopton memorial.

The restoration of the monument in 1749, when the substitution is supposed to have taken place, was recorded at the time in letters to a friend by the Reverend Joseph Greene, curate of Holy Trinity and master of the Grammar School. His letters come across as clear and honest, and indicate that he certainly believed the bust to be the original: 'The figure of the bard was taken down from his niche to be more commodiously cleansed from dust etc, and I can assure you that the bust and cushion [*sic*] before it is one entire limestone'; and 'care was taken, as nearly as could be, not to add to or diminish what the work consisted of, and appeared to have been when first erected. And really, except changing the substance of the architraves from alabaster to marble, nothing has been changed, nothing altered, except supplying with original material (saved for that purpose) whatsoever was by accident broken off, reviving the old colouring and renewing the gilding that was lost.' This same Joseph Greene also went to some pains to take a plaster cast of the bust before the restoration work in 1748, fearing that after the monument had been repaired no such close approach to it would be permitted.

A 1723 engraving of the memorial by George Vertue, published in Alexander Pope's 1725 edition of Shakespeare, is much closer to the monument as we know it, and its existence several years before the 1749 restoration argues against any major changes at that time. Moreover, Vertue also did a drawing of the monument *in situ* in the chancel in 1737. Hollar's engraving is therefore not the only pre-1749 source for what the monument actually looked like.

It is therefore more than likely that the monument in the church today is the one that was set up there some time between 1616 and 1623. There are, however, several questions raised by the monument and its inscription, which differs radically from the norm for the time. Unlike all the other epitaphs in Holy Trinity, Shakespeare is not given his first name, nor are there any mentions of his family: no 'husband of…' or 'father of…'. The last two lines giving his age and the date of his death appear very small and squashed. The corbels at the foot of the monument are rather stubby and small, unusual for a grand wall-mounted memorial. And perhaps most tellingly, 'envious death' cannot have 'plast' (placed) him in this monument, which is too small; nor is there a tomb 'decked' with his name. Altogether these anomalies seem to indicate that the memorial may originally have been intended to sit on top of

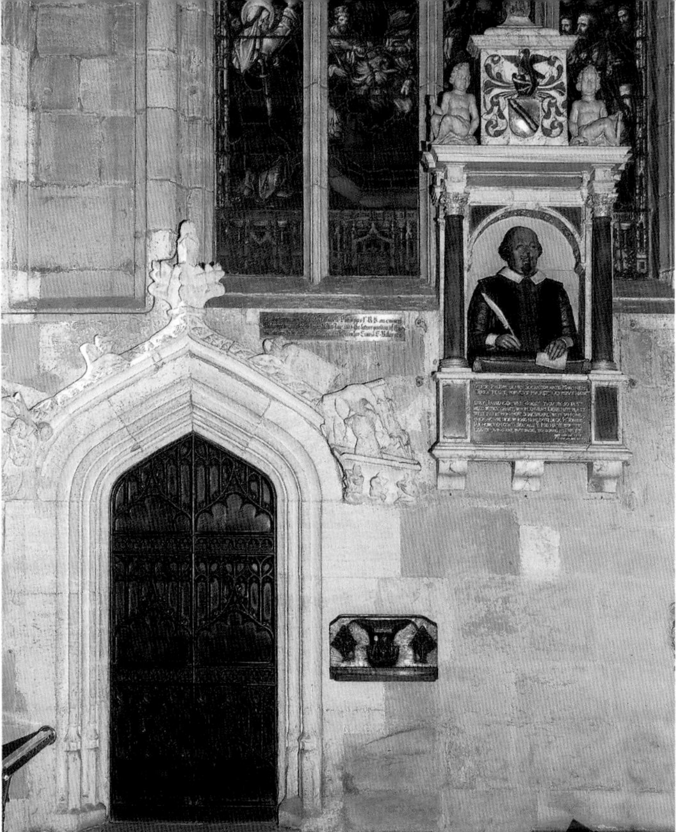

Right: The door which once led to the charnel house.

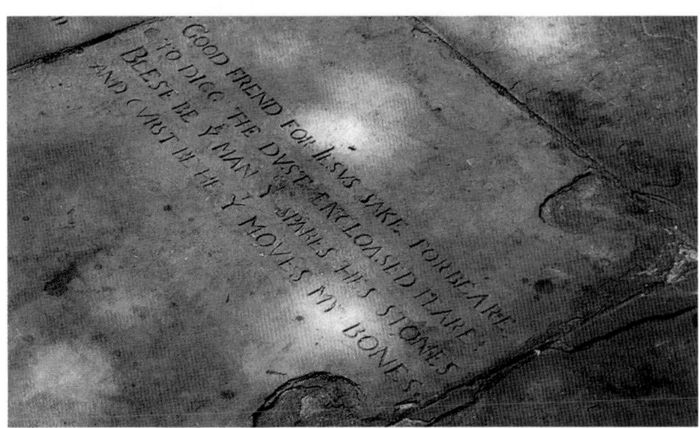

Below: Shakespeare's gravestone.

a much more elaborate tomb which would have carried a longer, more detailed and more informative epitaph. The assumption has to be that Shakespeare's final resting place was a job unfinished, for whatever reason. Ben Jonson's words echo that assumption: 'Thou art a memorial without a tomb'; and is it fanciful to read into Milton's encomium in the Second Folio a muted question about why the great poet and playwright does not have an equally distinguished memorial? Although kings might indeed wish to lie in the 'pomp' of Shakespeare's wonderful literary legacy, it was more usual at the time to commemorate great men more tangibly.

The gravestone

The sole inscription on Shakespeare's gravestone is:

> Good frend for Jesus sake forbeare
> To digg the dust encloased heare
> Bleste be ye man yt spares thes stones,
> And curst be he yt moves my bones

The lines are certainly early, as they were transcribed by Sir William Dugdale *c*1634, and were then published by Dugdale in 1656 in his *History and Antiquities of… Warwickshire*. They were also misquoted later in the century by Sir Francis Fane, and John Dowdall, a young barrister who was staying with a friend nearby, transcribed them in 1693 in a letter to his cousin, and added that the epitaph was 'made by himself a little before his death'.

Despite the lack of a name on the gravestone, Dugdale recorded the epitaph as indubitably belonging to the famous poet. But the grave, like the monument, raises questions. Why is it that Anne's grave takes pride of place directly under the monument, rather than William's, particularly since she died and was buried in 1623, seven years after her husband? And why is the poet's grave shorter, by some eighteen inches, than all the others in that row of graves in front of the chancel step?

The chancel has undergone much alteration since Shakespeare was buried there, and much may have happened to the gravestone which has gone unrecorded. It was not until the 1880s that the altar rails were moved out into the chancel, beyond the line of graves; before that, visitors freely stood and walked on the gravestones in order to get a good view of the monument. Protective measures were taken in the early nineteenth century to limit the damage that all those feet were causing. But it is possible that the original stone had become so worn that it was replaced, and re-engraved, at some stage during the three centuries following the burial. This was stated as fact in the late nineteenth century by the Shakespeare scholar J O Halliwell-Phillipps, and modern scholars support the idea. Stanley Wells has postulated that the family gravestones were moved at some point in their history, that Shakespeare's was placed nearer the altar and that it once carried a brass plaque, like Anne's. Such a plaque, like the quill on the memorial, could

Sir Walter Scott at Shakespeare's grave, a painting of 1828.

easily have fallen prey to a souvenir hunter. Martin Gorick feels, however, that the relatively poor state of Shakespeare's stone suggests that it is indeed the original, as a replacement would surely have been made to look more 'suitable' for one who was already so famous. The questions remain!

The Shakespeare Birthplace Trust owns a splendid oil painting, dated April 8 1828, of Sir Walter Scott reverently contemplating the grave (above). It shows him standing in a gloomy church with a shaft of light falling on the monument and the stone. There is a bunched-up cloth on Balsall's tomb, probably a carpet protecting Shakespeare's grave which had been removed so that Scott could see it. The step in front of the grave is damaged; and the gravestones themselves – those of William and Anne – are also rather battered about the edges. But the painting does seem to show them occupying the full space between the step down into the chancel and the step up to the altar beyond them; artistic license or an accurate rendition?

The Shakespeare family gravestones

The five members of the Shakespeare family whose gravestones lie in a row at the foot of the chancel steps, inside the altar rails, are, from left to right: Anne Shakespeare, William Shakespeare, Thomas Nash, who was the first husband of Shakespeare's granddaughter Elizabeth Hall, John Hall, husband of Shakespeare's daughter Susanna, and Susanna Hall. James Davenport, in his correspondence with the Shakespeare scholar Edmond Malone at the end of the eighteenth century, described Susanna's gravestone at that time as 'cut asunder' in the middle, and the 1836 plan of the chancel shows the name of Richard Watts inscribed on it. He was presumably a relative of the two members of the Watts family of Ryon Clifford who are buried in the two other graves in the sanctuary. Susanna's original epitaph had, luckily, been transcribed by William Dugdale, and it was recut on the stone in 1836.

It is unlikely that a row of grave plots in such a prominent position would have been reserved for members of the poet's family for the thirty-three years that elapsed between William's burial there in 1616 and Susanna's in 1649. Unless the gravestones were indeed moved to that position at some stage, it is perhaps more probable that there is a family vault underneath. There are other vaults beneath the chancel floor, for example the one dug for the Davenport family in the late eighteenth century, and more were recorded under the nave when heating pipes were being installed in the late nineteenth century. But unless further exploration is undertaken, such speculation will remain just that.

The monument and the gravestone – later history

The restoration in 1749 (see page 118) was the first recorded work on the monument, and arose from an unfavourable comparison of the Stratford bust with the new statue of Shakespeare recently erected in Westminster Abbey. A letter written by Joseph Greene in September 1746 refers to a performance of *Othello* by a company led by John Ward in the Town Hall, 'the profits arising from which… should be solely appropriated… to repairing the original monument of the poet'. This was in fact the first recorded staging of a Shakespeare play in Stratford. The money was handed over, but it was not until 1749 that the work was undertaken by John Hall of Bristol.

The next work done on the monument was the somewhat extraordinary agreement by James Davenport to the suggestion by Edmond Malone that the figure on the monument should be 'brought back to its original state by painting it a good stone-colour', apparently 'to suit the taste of the present age' (see pre-1835 watercolour, page 76). Davenport greatly regretted allowing this; according to his obituary, 'if there was any one circumstance connected with the memory of Shakespeare that ever caused him regret, it was his having allowed that miserable pretender to good taste, Malone, to disfigure the bust with the miserable coating of white paint, by which its original appearance is still hidden'.

Others clearly felt the same way, as an 1810 entry in the visitors' book reveals:

> Stranger to whom this monument is shown,
> Invoke the poet's curse upon Malone,
> Whose meddling zeal his barbarous taste betrays,
> And smears his tombstone as he marr'd his plays

There were proposals to remove the coating in 1818, amid much discussion as to whether it should be restored to the original colours or cleaned down to the stone and repainted. This did not happen, however, until 1861 when the work was undertaken by Simon Collins, supervised by the vicar George Granville, who testified, as the paint was removed, to 'the gradual development of the original colours'.

The inscriptions on the Shakespeare family gravestones

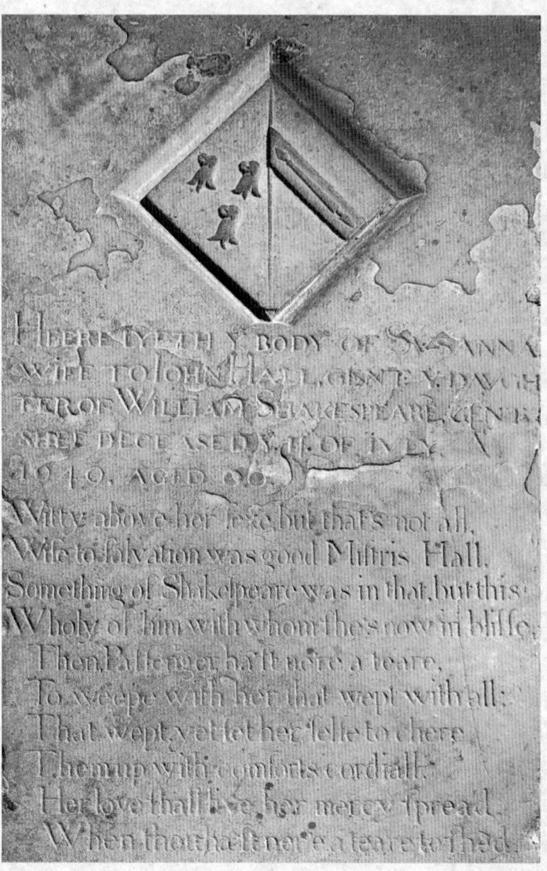

Epitaph of Susanna Hall, *née* Shakespeare, who died in 1649 at the age of sixty-six:

Heere lyes ye body of Susanna wife of John Hall
Gent, ye daughter of William Shakespeare gent.
She deceased ye 11th of July Ao 1649 aged 66

Witty above her sexe, but that's not all
Wise to salvation was good Mistris Hall
Something of Shakespeare was in that, but this
Wholey of him with whom she's now in blisse
Then, passenger, has't ne'er a teare
To weepe with her that wept with all
That wept, yet set herself to chere
Them up with comforts cordiall
Her love shall live, her mercy spread
When thou has't ne'er a teare to shed

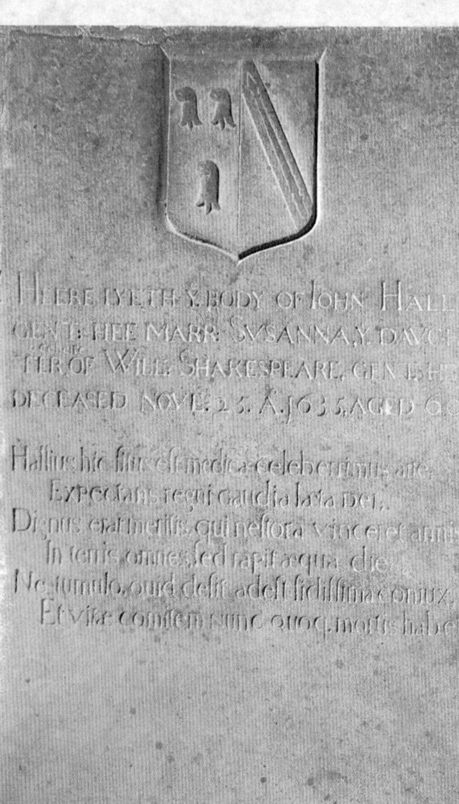

Epitaph of John Hall, Susanna Shakespeare's husband:

Heere lyeth the body of John Hall, Gent: he marr
Susanna, ye daughter and coheire of Will Shakespeare
Gent. Hee deceased Nover 25 Ao 1635 aged 60

Hallius hic situs est medica celeberrimus arte
Expectans regni gaudia laeta Dei
Dignus erat meritis qui nestora vinceret annis
In terris omnes sed rapit aequa dies
Ne tumulo, quid desit adest fidissima coniux
Et vitae comitem nunc quoq; mortis habet

Here is buried [John] Hall, most celebrated in the medical arts
In the hope of joyous happiness in the lord God
He was worthy of honour, who might have vanquished Nestor in years
But the unyielding day takes all men
Lest in the tomb he might want, his most faithful wife is now here
And he now has in death the companion of his life

Epitaph of Thomas Nash, first husband of Shakespeare's only granddaughter, Elizabeth Hall:

Heere resteth ye body of Thomas Nash Esq he mar
Elizabeth the daug and heire of John Halle gent.
He died Aprill 4 A 1647 aged 53

Fata manent omnes, hunc non virtute carentem
Ut neque divitiis, abstulit atra dies;
Abstulit; at referet lux ultima; siste viator,
Si peritura paras, per male parta peris

Death awaits all men; a black day has stolen away
One who was not lacking in virtue or riches
It has stolen him; the final light will bring him back
Stay, traveller; if you live for the moment, you die in misery

Epitaph of William Shakespeare:

Good frend for Jesus sake forbeare
To digg the dust encloased heare
Bleste be ye man yt spares thes stones,
And curst be he yt moves my bones

Epitaph of Anne Shakespeare, *née* Hathaway, who died in 1623 at the age of sixty-seven:

Ubera, tu mater, tu lac vitamque dedisti;
Vae mihi, pro tanto munere saxa dabo?
Quam mallem amoveat lapidem bonus angelus ore!
Exeat, ut Christi corpus, imago tua!
Sed nil vota valent; venias cito, Christe! Resurget
Clausa licet tumulo, mater et astra petet

Mother, you gave me the breast, you gave me milk and life;
Woe is me, that for so great a gift my return will be but a tomb
Would that the good angel would roll away the stone from its mouth!
And that your form, like the body of Christ, would come forth!
Yet my prayers are of no avail; come quickly, Christ!
That my mother, though shut in the tomb, may rise again and seek the stars

A drawing published in *The Times*, 1879, showing Edward, Prince of Wales, at Shakespeare's grave.

Collins touched up the paint where necessary, and the columns were repaired by 'Mr Vincent, sculptor of this town'. A newspaper article of the time made it clear that damage to the monument was not just the result of neglect; it seems that stonework within reach had been chipped off by 'sacrilegious visitors and senseless nonentities' who had also scribbled their names on the marble tablets by the inscriptions. Since the original stone pen had been repeatedly broken off, a real quill was placed in the bard's right hand. This used to be replaced annually on Shakespeare's birthday until the difficulty of sourcing suitable feathers ended this practice.

The most recent work on the poet's bust was undertaken in 1974 after vandals broke in one night and removed it from the memorial. It was found the following morning, lying damaged on the sanctuary floor; a finger and a cushion tassel were broken and there were several small scrapes and chips. The renovation was undertaken by Campbell, Smith & Co in their London studio. Their main aim was conservation of the original paintwork wherever possible, but it became clear that the damage would entail considerable repainting. The conservators therefore gently cleaned one side of the bust, and decided that, with careful touching up, the original paint on most of the head could be conserved and protected with a special varnish. A considerable amount of dirt was removed from the collar, but the cuff did not respond so well. The broken finger and tassel were repaired and remodelled, and the chips and scrapes made good. After the repairs were carried out, it was decided that the remainder of the figure would have to be repainted to restore the original seventeenth-century colours – though the colours are a little more subdued now than they would have originally appeared, in order to tone in better with the preserved paint on the head which ageing has now made darker.

The gravestone had never received the same attention as the monument, and had for centuries been casually walked over by visitors. Whether or not it was replaced in the mid-eighteenth century, by the 1830s concern was being expressed about its condition, and it was decided that the Shakespeare family stones should be covered with boards, with a trapdoor cut above the poet's grave which visitors could lift in order to read the inscription. One of the parish clerks also recorded later in the century that in 1844 the dirt that had accumulated in the letters of the inscription was removed and the letters themselves deepened 'most carefully and reverently' by the Reverend William Harness,

The story of Delia Bacon

Delia Bacon, an American, was a serious student of the works of Shakespeare, but became convinced that he could not possibly have written them himself, and believed that proof might be found in the grave.

In an article she published in *Putnam's Monthly* in January 1856, she set out her belief, arrived at through intensive study of the works themselves and using 'the commonest rules of historical investigation and criticism', that 'a drama more noble, and learned, and subtle than the Greek' could never have been 'the invention... of a stupid, ignorant, illiterate third-rate play-actor'. She was one of the first who believed that the true author must have been someone like Francis Bacon (no relation) or Walter Raleigh, or possibly both of them plus others.

The chancel in 1840.

Despite being in very poor health, she came to England to follow up her theories. In August 1856 she travelled from London to Leamington Spa, where she was so ill that the staff at her hotel did not expect her to last the night. However, she dragged herself on by coach to Stratford the next day (the train line to Stratford was not built until 1859), where she then stayed for several months, initially gathering her failing strength and then pursuing her specific aim of finding some evidence for her theories under the stone covering Shakespeare's grave, which she intended to prise up. When she felt strong enough, she visited Holy Trinity and spent time there familiarising herself with the layout of the chancel; but because of the constant streams of visitors, she was unable to make a solitary inspection of Shakespeare's gravestone and monument. She devoted herself instead to working up an acquaintance with the clerk, Thomas Kite, which eventually led to him agreeing to let her stay in the church after he had locked up for the night. On the appointed evening, she arrived at the church armed with implements with which she hoped to explore the grave; but she had promised the clerk that she would not do anything that might compromise him, so she went no further than making a preliminary examination. She then embarked on a correspondence with the vicar, George Granville, in the hope that he might be persuaded to go along with her plans. Rather oddly, he seems to have agreed that he would, at least in principle, provided that either he or the clerk should be involved.

But meanwhile she had found a publisher for the book she had written on her theories, which she wished to call *The Shakespeare Problem Solved*, and rumours were beginning to travel round Stratford that she was there to demolish the reputation of their favourite son. She decided that her plans would have to be put on hold; as she wrote in a letter of the time, 'The clerk of the parish and the vicar are both in my confidence. They know why I am here. But I must not speak of this at present. All that I can say is that the investigation which I came here to make is deferred.'

The book eventually came out with the title *The Philosophy of the Plays of Shakspere Unfolded*. But it did not receive the critical acclaim for which its author had hoped, and her mental health broke down completely; she had to be rescued by relatives from an asylum in Henley-on-Arden, and she returned to America where she died in 1859. Hers is a classic and sad case of misdirected intelligence. A kindly tribute to her, entitled 'Recollections of a gifted woman' and published in *The Atlantic Monthly* in 1863, gives Shakespeare the last word:

> No author had ever hoped so confidently as she; none ever failed more utterly. A superstitious fancy might suggest that the anathema on Shakespeare's tombstone had fallen heavily on her head in requital of even the unaccomplished purpose of disturbing the dust beneath, and that the 'Old Player' had kept so quietly in his grave, on the night of her vigil, because he foresaw how soon and terribly he would be avenged.

a guest at the time of the vicar, John Clayton. There is also an indication, in the painting of Sir Walter Scott at the grave, that a carpet was used to cover and protect the stones. The repositioning of the altar rails in the 1880s ultimately provided much more effective protection. However, the deterioration of the graves has continued, with the stone showing signs of shaling, and the church authorities are considering what remedial action to take.

Opening the grave

Tradition has it that Shakespeare composed his epitaph himself, inspired to do so by his horror of the charnel house. As he would certainly have known – and probably witnessed during his boyhood in the town – it was common practice to dig up the bones of earlier inhabitants of the graveyard to accommodate later burials, just as Yorick was – 'Alas, poor Yorick. I knew him, Horatio…' – to make way for Ophelia. When burial was the only church-sanctioned method of disposing of the dead, and sanctified ground for burials around churches rapidly became full, the ultimate resting place of the dead was as part of heaps of disarticulated bones within the charnel house – though those buried within the walls of the church usually escaped such a fate.

There is a report that the grave was in fact opened, or rather breached, in 1796 when a hole was knocked into it during the creation of a vault for Margaret Davenport, the wife of the vicar. When Washington Irving visited Stratford in 1815, he was told by the sexton that:

> A few years since… as some labourers were digging to make an adjoining vault, the earth caved in, so as to leave a vacant space almost like an arch through which one might have reached into his grave. No one, however, presumed to meddle with his remains, so awfully guarded by a malediction; and lest any of the idle or the curious, or any collector of relics, should be tempted to commit depredations, the old sexton kept watch over the place for two days, until the vault was finished and the aperture closed again. He told me he had made bold to look in at the hole, but could see neither coffin nor bones; nothing but dust…

The eighteenth century did see attempts to open Shakespeare's grave; some scholars thought that there might be manuscripts buried with the body, while others wanted his skull so that they might get a better idea of what he looked like. Horace Walpole is reported as offering 300 guineas for the skull, but refused to buy one produced in 1794 by a young doctor who claimed to have broken into the church to obtain it. That skull found a home in the vault of the Sheldon family in Beoley church.

It seems that the curse was working its magic, because no serious attempts appear to have been made on the grave – until, that is, the arrival on the scene in the 1850s of an extraordinary American woman, Delia Bacon (see box, page 125). But it is also true that the revenues raised from visitors to the literary shrine were important to the church, and the cult status now adhering to the tomb would clearly be irrevocably damaged if it were to be opened and nothing found. When opening the tomb was raised in 1876, the incumbent's unequivocal answer was that 'the persons proposing such an experiment would have to walk over my prostrate body'. A proposal in 1883 that there should be an archaeological investigation of grave and monument was met by an admission by George Arbuthnot, the vicar, that he would not oppose it if public opinion overwhelmingly supported it. The misreporting of this qualified response as his support for the scheme led to such a volley of abusive letters that the idea was taken no further.

Since then, proposals to open the grave have come mainly from avowed Baconians who wish to find out, once and for all, whether there are any manuscripts there. Incumbents (and Home Secretaries) have invariably, and vigorously, turned down these approaches; one in the 1960s was met by Thomas Bland, the vicar, with the forceful response, 'Even if I were given proof that there were manuscripts inside, even if my bishop were in favour, even if I had to stand up to the whole world – I would not allow the tomb to be disturbed.' It remains untouched.

CELEBRATIONS OF SHAKESPEARE

In 1769 the Town Council invited David Garrick, the foremost Shakespearian actor of his day, to organise a celebration of the poet. Known as the Shakespeare Jubilee, it attracted visitors from all over the country. On the first morning, the mayor and Corporation, together with Garrick and other distinguished guests, made their way to the church where Thomas Arne conducted a performance of his oratorio *Judith*. Many of the audience stayed at the end of the piece to pay homage to the Shakespeare memorial, which had been hidden from them during the performance by the orchestra gathered in the chancel. Those returning later in the day found that Mrs Garrick and one of the singers had festooned it with flowers and foliage, to the extent that the correspondent from *Gentleman's Magazine* thought that it looked 'more like the god Pan than Shakespeare'.

This was the precursor of regular celebrations in Stratford of Shakespeare as a literary figure. In 1824, for the first time, the newly formed Shakespeare Club (which still flourishes) marked the poet's birthday on April 23 with a ceremonial dinner, and the tercentenary of his birth in 1864 was the occasion for a major festival in the town, within which religious services in the church were included for the first time. The vicar, George Granville, was heavily involved with the planning of this event. George Arbuthnot encouraged the revival of the birthday celebrations, instituting a short address at the grave on the day itself and inviting eminent preachers to deliver a 'Shakespeare sermon' on the Sunday nearest to the day.

The Birthday weekend is now a highlight of the Stratford year. On the Saturday nearest to April 23 a great procession of bands, dancers, actors, clergy, townspeople and schoolchildren all make their way to the church, all carrying flowers. The vicar and the church staff meet them at the altar rail and cover the sanctuary with a carpet of blossoms, which look wonderful and scent the air unforgettably. The boys from King Edward VI School always lead the procession and rosemary is worn for remembrance, as offered by Ophelia in *Hamlet*. In 1896 the American ambassador was invited to attend, and since then many international diplomats have joined the people of Stratford in celebrating the poet, with their many flags adding to the grandeur of the occasion.

The church is always packed on the Sunday of the Birthday weekend for the special service, when actors and musicians of the Royal Shakespeare Company take part and a distinguished speaker preaches. There are other events too: a formal lunch, a Birthday Performance at the theatre and lots of street entertainment.

There's rosemary, that's for remembrance.

(HAMLET, 4.5)

The 2009 Birthday celebrations

Left: Two preachers of the Shakespeare Sermon: Paul Edmondson (2005) and Paula Byrne (2008), in the Birthday procession.

Right: The Bishop of Coventry and Sir Donald Sinden.

Centre right: The Band of the Royal Engineers beating the retreat.

Below: People dressed as William and Anne Shakespeare laying flowers at the grave.

This was one of the most exuberant yet. Sir Donald Sinden officiated at the opening ceremony, when excerpts from *As You Like It* were read by an RSC actor and two local schoolboys. The people's procession featured the roar of motor bikes as well as skateboarders, marching bands, belly dancers, morris dancers, Tudor characters, giant puppets and foreign dignitaries, all following a new route from the Birthplace to Holy Trinity church. The grave and the chancel disappeared under hundreds of floral tributes. There was even a reproduction in flowers of the Cobbe portrait of Shakespeare, which was on exhibition at the Shakespeare Centre. Passengers on the chain ferry across the Avon were entertained with sonnets read by RSC actors and visitors to all the Shakespeare houses were offered a complimentary slice of birthday cake. There were workshops run by members of the RSC in the intricacies of stage combat and dance, and across the region other events were staged, making the Birthday an event spreading its wings beyond Stratford.

Now, my fair'st friend,
I would I had some flowers o'th'
spring that might
Become your time of day.
(THE WINTER'S TALE, 4.4)

Above: The making of a likeness in flowers of the newly discovered Cobbe portrait.

Left: Katy Stephens and Mariah Gale of the RSC in 'Shakespeare Remembered' at the Shakespeare Service, 2009.

5 THE CHURCH TODAY

What a piece of work is a man! How noble in reason, how infinite in faculty.

(HAMLET, 2.2)

Any parish church in the country which can lay claim to 800 and more years of history – as many of them, like Holy Trinity, can – is able to stand proudly beside the great cathedrals and minsters and abbey churches in celebrating its continuous and continuing role in the worship of God. These buildings resonate with history and tradition. They have echoed with the happiness wrought by new babies and new marriages, and with the mourning of the bereaved. They have witnessed vicious clashes as old religious practices have given way to new ideas, and have seen their walls and windows, their monuments and decorations demolished, altered and added to as beliefs and fashions have changed.

Today, too, they have additional challenges to face, in the increasing secularisation of society and the lessening of the traditional deference towards establishment bodies which have between them led to fallings off in both the belief in and practice of religion. Congregations have dwindled as Sundays have become just another day in the week and leisure pursuits like shopping and sport have offered alternatives to what used to be central and special to the Sabbath. The church may still be Established, but its relevance to today's society often has to be defended and justified.

Yet Holy Trinity has weathered these storms, and can boast high attendance at its services and a flourishing range of activities in which the members of its congregation of all ages eagerly participate. To quote Sir Brian Follett, chair of the Friends of Shakespeare's Church, Holy Trinity is 'a roaring success'. And although the Shakespeare connection has a lot to contribute, not least through the support and help offered by distinguished actors who are playing at the theatres, it is only part of the story. Holy Trinity's good fortune is to have a devoted band of clergy and lay staff, led by Martin Gorick, who are unstinting in their work for the building and those who worship in it, as well as for those who visit it mainly for its famous resident. It is truly a flourishing modern church which offers a huge range of services – religious and secular – to the town and the townspeople.

MUSIC

We know that Holy Trinity had four choristers from the late fifteenth century on, and we also know that it had two organs, since Richard Sharpe, *pulsator organorum*, had a yearly stipend of £6 granted to him by the king on the dissolution of the college at the Reformation. But fifty or so years later choristers and organs were gone, and music in the church would then have consisted of the unaccompanied hymn singing of the congregation in unison, led by the clerk. A church like Holy Trinity may have been able to call on the services of a violinist or flautist; but it was not until the middle of the eighteenth century that the church again acquired an organ.

Opposite: Holy Trinity's music director, Andrew Jones, wearing 'rosemary for remembrance' on Shakespeare's birthday.

The newly cleaned and polished organ, 2010.

Choral music as we now understand it began to be heard again in Holy Trinity at the beginning of the nineteenth century, and has been a part of worship in the church ever since. Until very recently it was male voice only; but today's choir is a mixture of men and women, girls and boys from Stratford and local villages.

For services the choir wear red robes with surplices, and ruffs for the trebles, and they sing from the choir stalls at the east end of the nave. The repertoire is a traditional one, drawing on church music from the sixteenth to the twentieth century. The choir are on duty at Sunday morning services, when the congregation joins in for some of the music, and

Is this still an active church?

This question is frequently asked of the church staff who man the shop and the pay point in the nave where those who wish to visit Shakespeare's grave in the chancel are asked to make their donation. It is one that particularly exercises Jon Ormrod, the head verger, whose job of running the church day-to-day is balanced by what he sees as his 'visitor ministry'.

He has a tourist's itinerary to contend with. The average amount of time spent in the church by a 'Shakespeare visitor' is around four minutes – a dash through to the chancel, a look at the memorial, the family gravestones and the font, maybe time to read the baptism record and then taking and posing for photographs, before it's back to all the other tourist attractions Stratford has to offer, perhaps via the church shop by the porch door.

There are, however, many visitors who also stop to look at the church itself: the misericords, the Clopton Chapel, the sanctuary knocker, the stained glass (if they don't sniff at it as 'only Victorian'). A volunteer guide in the chancel may point out the vernicle, and those who enjoy medieval churches will take time to admire Balsall's tomb, the sedilia and what is left of the carvings above the doors.

But Holy Trinity is indeed still an active church, and still carries out the function for which it was built centuries ago – the daily worship of God.

For the church staff, it is a bonus if at least some visitors pause to sit and contemplate for a while, or maybe kneel in prayer in St Peter's Chapel in the south transept, which is set aside for private worship and is where daily prayers are held each morning. It is their aim to persuade visitors to see Holy Trinity not just as a building with a famous grave in it but as a place which can provide an oasis of spiritual peace within a busy tourist's day.

The kneelers

Will Hawkes, a retired architect, and an active member of Holy Trinity's congregation since the 1970s, was the power behind the project to design and embroider a whole new set of kneelers for the church. There was a strong feeling that they should reflect the Christian tradition rather than the Shakespearian connection, and so he suggested that they should be based on the *Benedicite*, a canticle used in morning prayer which calls on all the powers and elements of heaven and earth to 'bless the Lord; praise him and magnify him for ever'; '*Benedicite, omnia opera Domini, Domino; laudate et superexaltate eum in saecula*'.

He therefore drew up a set of designs using the imagery from the canticle – the waters above the firmament, the sun and moon, the stars of heaven, the showers and dew, the winds, the seasons, fire and heat, night and day, light and darkness, frost and cold, mountains and hills, whales, fowl, beasts and cattle... – and made up embroidery patterns from them.

The church then recruited a team of embroiderers, who included both those experienced in the craft and relative beginners, which meant that the designs too had to be manageable across a range of skills. There were eventually around forty volunteers for the task who came from a wide variety of walks of life and locations, including a man who lived in Canada; and the work took over twenty years to complete. The kneelers they embroidered now adorn the pews and are in constant use during services.

Work is now ongoing on new designs for choir seats based on Psalm 150 and using text and musical notes.

Forever will I kneel upon my knees.
(*RICHARD II*, 5.3)

also at choral evensong. They are well used to singing before large audiences: the numbers attending services at Holy Trinity are high, particularly on special feast days such as Good Friday and Easter Day, and can number several hundred for events like Shakespeare Sunday, Remembrance Sunday, midnight mass and the Christmas carol service when over 700 attend.

The choir also perform elsewhere, sometimes deputising for cathedral choirs – they have visited Exeter, Lincoln and Coventry Cathedrals in this capacity – and have travelled abroad; they visited Tuscany in 2008 and New York and Boston in 2010.

Andrew Jones, who joined Holy Trinity as music director in 2006, has encouraged other types of music in the church as well as the choral repertoire. As part of a family service on the first Sunday of each month, the Music Group from the congregation, led by Nik Rothwell, lead more contemporary music. On special occasions Mrs Rothwell's two daughters – a talented violinist and cellist – have played with the choir, and the services of accomplished trumpeters can also be called on at times when fanfares are required.

Holy Trinity church as a concert venue is much in demand; it hosts hundreds of informal concerts from visiting choirs, and is regularly used by local musical groups such as the Stratford Choral Society, the Chamber Choir and the St James Singers. There is an annual young persons' concert which provides an opportunity for singers and musicians from local schools to perform in a beautiful and historic building, and a series of lunchtime organ recitals in summer, as well as events like piano masterclasses and festal evensongs, often accompanied by sandwiches or followed by supper.

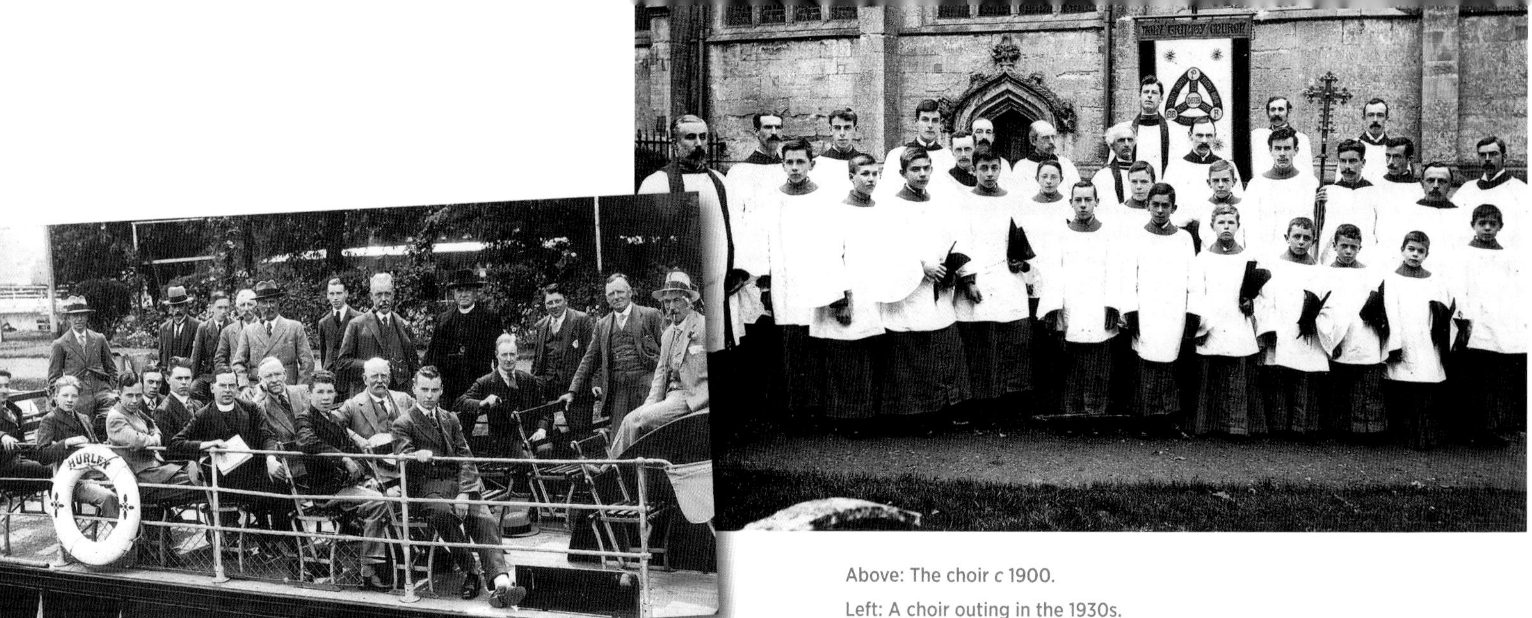

Above: The choir *c* 1900.
Left: A choir outing in the 1930s.

Much of this activity is sponsored and organised by the Friends of the Music, who are also involved with the social side of music at Holy Trinity. They arrange a weekend away each year, for example to Canterbury or York, where musical and religious pursuits can be enjoyed along with the usual tourist attractions. The Friends also act as front of house for the concerts and other musical events that take place in the church; and they are active and successful fundraisers, raising money for new equipment such as the chamber organ they bought in 2008.

HISTORY OF THE CHOIR

Tim Raistrick

Ralph Collingwood, later Dean of Lichfield, provided an endowment for four choristers to assist daily at Matins and Vespers. Choristers continued to be used over the coming centuries, although the changing styles of service required similar changes both in the music and in the places in the church where they sang.

The formation of the sort of choir that now sings in Holy Trinity can be traced back to the 1830s; a chorister who later became choirmaster was Thomas Helmore, a talented tenor and composer. In 1836 he founded and was the first conductor of the Stratford Choral Society, and he went on to be choirmaster at the Chapel Royal where he was a huge influence on Arthur Sullivan, then a boy chorister.

It was at the consecration service to mark a major internal reordering of the church in 1854 that the choir first appeared in cassock and surplice; this caused, it was noted at the time, considerable amazement among the congregation. Under the care of George Arbuthnot, the choir flourished. Choral evensong was sung daily and a choir school was established, although it only survived for nine years. A photograph from around 1900 (above) indicates that the choir at that time had around thirty members.

Although the choir did not admit girls until 1993, charity girls had sung at services a couple of hundred years earlier, and even in Arbuthnot's time a group of Sunday school girls was asked to lead the singing at one service each month.

Although the adult singers have never been paid, the junior choristers were always regarded as professional musicians and received remuneration for their services. In the late 1890s it was noted by the vicar in the parish magazine that a boy who was in the choir for six years would earn £23 10s over this period – a sizeable amount in those days.

Other ways of rewarding the choir have been annual outings. In the Victorian period these would be to places such as Blenheim Palace; but one such trip allowed some of the men of the choir to make a detour to inspect a sewage works, which was then something of a novelty. In the 1960s, trips further afield were arranged, one being to Heathrow Airport to watch the planes. In the 1970s, London was the favourite destination, with a lunch in a private dining room at the Victoria and Albert Museum starting the visit. Nowadays, theme parks such as Drayton Manor are preferred.

Concerts have been a regular part of the choir's output. Some of these have been fundraising events for the choir itself, for example for the 2008 trip to Italy, while others have been to raise money for local good causes or to celebrate particular occasions; in the 1970s, for example, the choir was invited to sing a concert to celebrate the restoration of the organ at Streatley-on-Thames.

The choir has played an important role in the diocese, taking part in the first performance of Britten's *War Requiem*

at the opening of Coventry Cathedral in 1962, and has broadcast regularly on television and radio, particularly in the 1980s and 1990s. A record was made in the 1960s and the choir performed alongside the voices of actors such as Laurence Olivier in a *Son et Lumière* at the church in 1970 (see page 140). For many years, the choir was a regular source of boy actors for the Royal Shakespeare Company, mirroring the ancient practice of the theatre using singers in this way.

One of the most unusual things the choir used to do was to help open the Steam Fair (similar to the October Mop Fair, but with steam-driven rides), which in the 1970s was held on land where the Holiday Inn now stands and then on the old station site at the end of New Street. A service would be held with the choir and clergy standing on the steps of one of the rides and the hymns accompanied by a steam organ. Afterwards, still wearing full robes, the choir and braver clergy got free rides – a remarkable sight!

Above: The choir today.

Left and below: The choir at the Steam Fair, 1973.

The choir school

When George Arbuthnot arrived as vicar in 1879 he began to explore the idea of rewarding service in the choir with free education. He was keen to recruit boys of 'good social standing' for the choir, because he hoped to get rid of the strong local accent that he felt sometimes 'marred the singing'. By 1881 he was able to open a choir school, headed by Mr J A Priest, which had so grown in numbers a year later that an assistant master had to be engaged.

Those accepted as choristers received free education for a year, after which, if their voices and conduct were good enough, they were awarded choral scholarships which would last until their voices broke. Parents had to undertake not to remove them from the school while they could still sing as trebles, and to allow them to perform whenever the vicar required them.

Unfortunately, this generous arrangement fell victim to conflict between the vicar and the headmaster. The causes of the 'disagreeable friction' were not reported, but in 1890 it was announced in the parish magazine that 'A dual authority never works well' and that the vicar had removed his choristers from Mr Priest's school and arranged for them to join the Grammar School.

THE BELLS

The first record of bells in the tower is from 1502 when a legacy of 6s 8d (33p) was left towards their restoration, though nothing is known of their number or weights at that time. In 1552, at the end of the reign of Edward VI, two of the bells were sold because they were cracked, with the money going towards the maintenance of the bridge, and five bells from the dismantled Abbey of Hailes were purchased from the Crown at the cost of £75. Part of this cost was defrayed by the sale, for at least £61, of further old bells to a number of Stratford townspeople, and the vicar, Roger Dyos, contributed 20s to the purchase of the new bells, as did Edward Alcock, sub-warden of the college, who gave 8s.

These bells would have been familiar to William Shakespeare; they appear in *As You Like It* (2.5):

> If ever you have looked on better days,
> If ever been where bells have knolled to church.

and in Sonnet 71:

> ... the surly sullen bell
> Give warning to the world that I am fled.

They marked the town's events, being used to summon the townspeople to council meetings and sermons, giving the alarm when a fire broke out, tolling for death and burial and acting as the town's clock. The Guild Chapel also had bells, though not in Shakespeare's time. One of them was hung there as a curfew bell in 1633, and still rings the curfew at 8pm every day; the other was a fire bell, hung in 1782 when part of the Guildhall was in use as a fire station. Both were rehung in 1992.

In October 1617 the Holy Trinity churchwardens reported that 'we were cited to Worcester because the bells were out of order', and presumably as a result, in December of that year, £4 12d (£4.05) was paid for recasting. Three decades later, in 1650, a vestry minute records that 'It was agreed upon that there shall be a levy made for the gathering of £10 viz £5 for the town and £5 for the parish to cast three new bells'. These presumably formed part of the ring of six of which some were cast by Henry and Matthew Bagley between 1683 and 1742. Two new trebles were added in 1887 to celebrate Queen Victoria's golden jubilee, and at the same time the third and fourth of the existing six were recast and all the bells rehung.

Above and right: Bells old and new, 1948.

The metal from this ring of eight was used in 1948 to produce a new complete ring of ten, hung on a new metal frame. The work was done by Taylors of Loughborough, and the result was that the Stratford bells are arguably one of the best light rings of ten in existence. Inscriptions from the old bells were retained wherever possible. The first full peal of Grandsire Caters was rung on these new bells in February 1949.

In 1994 an additional bell was installed alongside the ringing peal to act as a service and Sanctus bell. Cast by Warners in 1881, it hung in the town cemetery chapel until the building fell out of use, when it was donated to the church by the Town Council. The church also possesses an Ellacombe device, a chiming mechanism which allows one or two people to play tunes on the bells. This equipment is used when there are not enough ringers available to form a team.

Ringers and ringing

The current tower captain is Charles Wilson who has held the position for some twenty-five years, having joined the Holy Trinity team when he came to live in Stratford in the mid-1970s. His deputy, who does most of the training of new ringers, is Bill Hicks, who has recruited an enthusiastic group of young people from King Edward VI Grammar School and Shottery Girls Grammar School into the ringing team – new blood offering, it is hoped, a sound foundation for the future.

A great deal of commitment is needed. Not only are there the weekly Sunday morning services to attend, but there is also a weekly practice on Tuesday evenings, as well as weddings and the occasional funeral. Early attendance is required on Ascension Day, when the bells are rung from 6.50am to 7.30am for the early parish Eucharist. And some members of the team regularly visit other local churches such as those at Chipping Campden, Welford-on-Avon, Clifford Chambers and Luddington.

The church also welcomes visiting ringers, who flock to Holy Trinity because of the excellence of the bells – though the position of the church within a residential community limits the number of occasions on which peals and quarters can be rung. Full peals – which take around three hours – are rung only three times a year; they and the more frequent quarter peals celebrate major events, anniversaries or significant national and local occasions. A quarter peal of Grandsire Doubles was rung on June 6 1994 to commemorate the fiftieth anniversary of D-Day, for example; and in 2009 the Durham University Society of Change Ringers celebrated their fiftieth anniversary by ringing a full peal of Stedman Caters, consisting of 5040 changes.

Son et Lumière

Stratford-upon-Avon 1970

CAST

IN ORDER OF APPEARANCE.

Prologue (*The Tempest*)	RALPH RICHARDSON
Narrator	IAN RICHARDSON
Bible	PAUL SCOFIELD
Berhtwulf	ANDREW CRUICKSHANK
Monks & Builders	NORMAN RODWAY
Workmen & Clerks	RICHARD RYDER
Assayer	JASON MATHEWS
Judge	NORMAN RODWAY
John Shakespeare	PATRICK BARR
Mary Shakespeare	BRENDA BRUCE
Dogberry	NORMAN RODWAY
Seacole	IAN RICHARDSON
When in disgrace with fortune . . .	JOHN GIELGUD
O, monstrous, monstrous . . .	RALPH RICHARDSON
Fear no more . . .	EDITH EVANS
Let me not to the marriage of the minds . . .	LAURENCE OLIVIER
That time of year . . .	PAUL SCOFIELD
William Shakespeare	LAURENCE OLIVIER
Sweet Swan of Avon . . .	ANTHONY QUAYLE
Vicar	PATRICK BARR
Citizen	JUDI DENCH
David Garrick	PAUL SCOFIELD
Not marble nor the guilded monuments . . .	PEGGY ASHCROFT

DRAMA

It is inevitable that the last resting place of one of the greatest playwrights the world has ever seen should host dramatic productions, and that the great actors who come to Stratford to play the timeless roles that he created should lend their presence and their expertise to some of the drama that takes place at Holy Trinity. A notable example in recent years of this collaboration between church and theatre was the summer 2006 production of *Henry VIII* in Holy Trinity as

The Holy Trinity production of Henry VIII

As one approached the building along the tree-lined avenue, one had an excited feeling of anticipation. We were to see one of Shakespeare's history plays enacted in an arena rich itself in church history and drama. It did not matter that debate still continues as to whether John Fletcher wrote some of it, for this enthralling production by the company AandBC, under the splendid direction of Gregory Thompson, confirmed that the play itself was indeed the thing.

The audience were admitted through the great west door and sat on either side of the majestic nave facing the spectators on the opposite side. Such a transverse setting proved a masterstroke, for not only did the stained glass windows provide a striking and colourful background to the action, but the latter itself swiftly unfolded along the whole of the nave with the acting company moving up and down, not only like pawns in a political/ecclesiastical game but players in a tournament of plot and counter-plot.

The company were only fifteen in number, but between them they recreated with great panache the many roles in the cast list. One was able to concentrate on the words and enjoy the way we, the audience, were invited to be onlookers as the Duke of Buckingham addressed us prior to his execution, guests at Wolsey's banquet and spectators at the court hearing to bring about a royal divorce. The latter scene was particularly effective as Henry selected audience members at random to confide in as members of the bench of bishops. At the performance I attended, my neighbour who was thus involved was none other than Clifford Rose, a founder member of the RSC. This entertaining device continued in the second half as we were invited to eavesdrop on court gossip, become the rude multitude outside the royal palace and finally share the celebrations at the christening of the Princess Elizabeth.

The costumes designed by Ellen Cairns were both in period and magnificent. The impressive music composed by David Stoll was provided by Christopher Goodwin (lute/percussion) and Holy Trinity's former director of music, Peter Summers (organ). And the performances themselves? Truly memorable, especially from the main protagonists – Antony Byrne in the title role, Corinne Jaber as Katherine of Aragon, Aoife McMahon as Anne Bullen, Anthony O'Donnell as Cardinal Wolsey, Derek Hutchinson as Buckingham and Jem Wall as Archbishop Cranmer. And these were just the pick of a remarkably fine bunch of actors.

As the play drew to a close with the Reformation in England now certain and unstoppable, one could not but reflect that this significant time in the history of the English church was captured forever in the spiritual setting that is Holy Trinity. The action of the text might have ended, but we were left with evidence of the Reformation all around us. The words of Shakespeare/Fletcher had given us much to reflect on – and Shakespeare's church, where we had listened to those words, was there to make us think even more.

Far left: Flyer and cast list for *Son et Lumière*, 1970.

Left: Rehearsing for the opening recital of the 1977 Stratford-upon-Avon Poetry Festival, July 10 1977. Left to right: Peter Pears, John Strickson, Princess Grace of Monaco, John Westbrook, Richard Pasco.

part of the 'Complete Works' festival of Shakespeare, which took some of the productions outside the theatre to other venues (see box). And the building itself has been the inspiration for dramatic pieces specifically written to be performed within its walls. One of these was *Bare Ruined Choirs*, taking its title from Sonnet 73, written by Greg Doran of the RSC and enacted at Holy Trinity on November 25 2007. A compendium of readings and music, it brought together the threads of the history of the church as it impinged on Shakespeare's life and work, and was performed in the candlelit church by Greg Doran himself along with Dame Judi Dench, Sir Antony Sher and Jeffery Dench, accompanied by the Armonico Consort.

The church and the parish hall are also heavily used by local groups, who take advantage of Holy Trinity's dramatic credentials as a stepping stone towards their own creations and their own interpretations of a wide variety of productions. There are two drama groups within the Holy Trinity community: Nova Theatre Group, run by Jon and Sheonagh Ormrod, mainly for young people, and the Trinity Players, run by Ursula Russell and Tony Boyd-Williams.

Antony Byrne as Henry VIII, in *Henry VIII at Holy Trinity*, by AandBC; part of the RSC Complete Works Festival, 2006.

Holy Trinity itself was used to provide spectacle, with the west door flung open to show a stunning firework display during the feasting at the cardinal's palace, and the font used for the baptism of the baby Elizabeth. Several real babies were used during the run of the play. At the end of the evening, the west door was flung open once more to enable us to depart, each audience member being presented with a wrapped comfit to celebrate the royal occasion we had just seen enacted. As we made our way back along the path, the bells of the church rang out a triumphant peal to continue the royal celebrations. Henry's closing words seemed so appropriate:

> This little one shall make it a holiday.

I am sure all who witnessed such a splendid piece of theatre in such a splendid setting were indeed in a holiday humour.

Tony Boyd-Williams

Happy Birthday William! Head verger, Jon Ormrod, lights the candles at the end of 'Coffee, cake and sonnets', readings to celebrate Shakespeare's Birthday, 2009.

Jon and Sheonagh Ormrod are highly experienced former stage managers, and now bring their theatrical experience to their youth drama group. In 2001 they had the idea of putting on a performance of *Joseph and the Amazing Technicolour Dreamcoat*. They were very fortunate to be joined by Jenny Barrie as their musical director and the three of them have worked together on several of their productions. Nova's principal aim is to enable all children to be involved in putting on a show, and from there encourage them, if possible, to get involved in church activities. Nova believes that with any group activity the whole is often greater than the sum of the individual parts. Nowhere is that more evident than in a theatrical production, where all children have a talent to contribute to the final performance. Nova welcomes all children who wish to be part of their shows, with the aim that they all learn to work with each other, build their confidence and discover some of the skills required to mount a production. The only auditions are those to determine individual parts and there is no cost, although everyone is encouraged to take part in fundraising.

Since the initial production of *Joseph*, Nova have put on four other musicals, transforming the hall in the Parish Centre opposite the church during February half term into a theatre space using professional lighting and sound equipment and aiming for production standards that are as high as possible. A growing tradition in the shows has been a full company dance number choreographed by Nik Rothwell, leader of Holy Trinity Music Group and a highly skilled practitioner. Jon and Sheonagh Ormrod feel very lucky to have worked with the adult members of the cast, who have been very generous in all they have bought to their shows, and are hugely grateful to Jenny Barrie, Andrew Jones and Nik

Holy Trinity's links with the Royal Shakespeare Company

I have been Theatre Chaplain for the RSC in Stratford since 2002 and very much value my contact with such a creative group of people who are also one of Stratford's biggest employers. Their annual carol service is held at Holy Trinity and they join us for the Shakespeare Service around Shakespeare's birthday each year. Many actors and other members of the company have found their spiritual home at Holy Trinity, and do to this day.

Martin Gorick

Ever since 1622, when Shakespeare's old company, on tour in the West Midlands, arrived in Stratford to view the funerary bust of their great friend and playwright, actors have made the pilgrimage to Holy Trinity to pay their respects. The King's Men were paid six shillings by the town Corporation not to perform that day. Luckily, Stratford eventually saw fit to honour their local boy, and when the first Memorial Theatre opened in 1879, Helen Faucit, playing Beatrice in the birthday performance of *Much Ado*, was allowed within the altar rails to gaze on that famous domed brow. She said, 'The bust looks like a living friend, whom one would wish never to part with'. Perhaps it's that sentiment that keeps me coming back to spend a few minutes in the church, in quiet contemplation of the gentle genius who gave us all those words; who had the wit to say, as Alexander Pope wrote, 'what oft was thought, but ne'er so well expressed'. Lingering in the chancel among the carved misericords in the choir stalls, I often wonder how Shakespeare knew me so well, how he manages to see us from all 360 degrees. He illuminates our understanding of mankind, and to me too, he seems like a living friend.

Gregory Doran, Chief Associate Director, Royal Shakespeare Company

Joe Millson, Harriet Walter and Sir Patrick Stewart in a Friends fundraiser held in Holy Trinity in autumn 2008.

Nova Theatre Group: above, rehearsing *Godspell*, 2010; left, *The Wizard of Oz*, 2006.

The Trinity Players: top left, the poster for *Barchester Towers*, 2009; far left, *Toad of Toad Hall*, 2008.

Rothwell for their time and talent. But the main reward has been the young people and the wonderful energy and commitment they all bring to each production.

The Trinity Players offer more frequent dramatic events, some of them forming part of worship, particularly on festal occasions during the church year, and some taking the form of quite low-key 'happenings' in the church. One of these is 'Coffee, cake and sonnets' on Shakespeare's birthday, when coffee and cake are offered in the former chapel of St Thomas of Canterbury in the south aisle, accompanied by the reading of Shakespeare's sonnets and other extracts from his works. This has become a popular event, attended both by parishioners and by tourists who stop to see what is going on and stay to join in.

Formed in 2007, the Trinity Players' repertoire includes rehearsed readings, adaptations of literary works and dramatic readings during or in place of services. Actors who worship at Holy Trinity when playing with the RSC have taken part in some of these readings. The group's facilitators, Ursula Russell and Tony Boyd-Williams, who both have backgrounds in drama and are skilled in adaptation and staging, delight in the creative scope and space offered by Holy Trinity church: a robed figure singing in the crossing, a disembodied voice from the organ loft high in the roof of the nave, the great west door flung wide for a troupe of dancers, a 'sermon' from the pulpit lit only by candles, stone pillars for lurking lovers and villains. Drawing on a large and remarkably talented congregation of all ages from babies to sprightly octogenarians, the Players now have a wide repertoire, which includes productions that are not specifically religious and welcomes original writing. Trinity Players is a group with a difference, drawing strength and inspiration both from the beautiful historic building and from the multifarious talents of Holy Trinity's vibrant congregation.

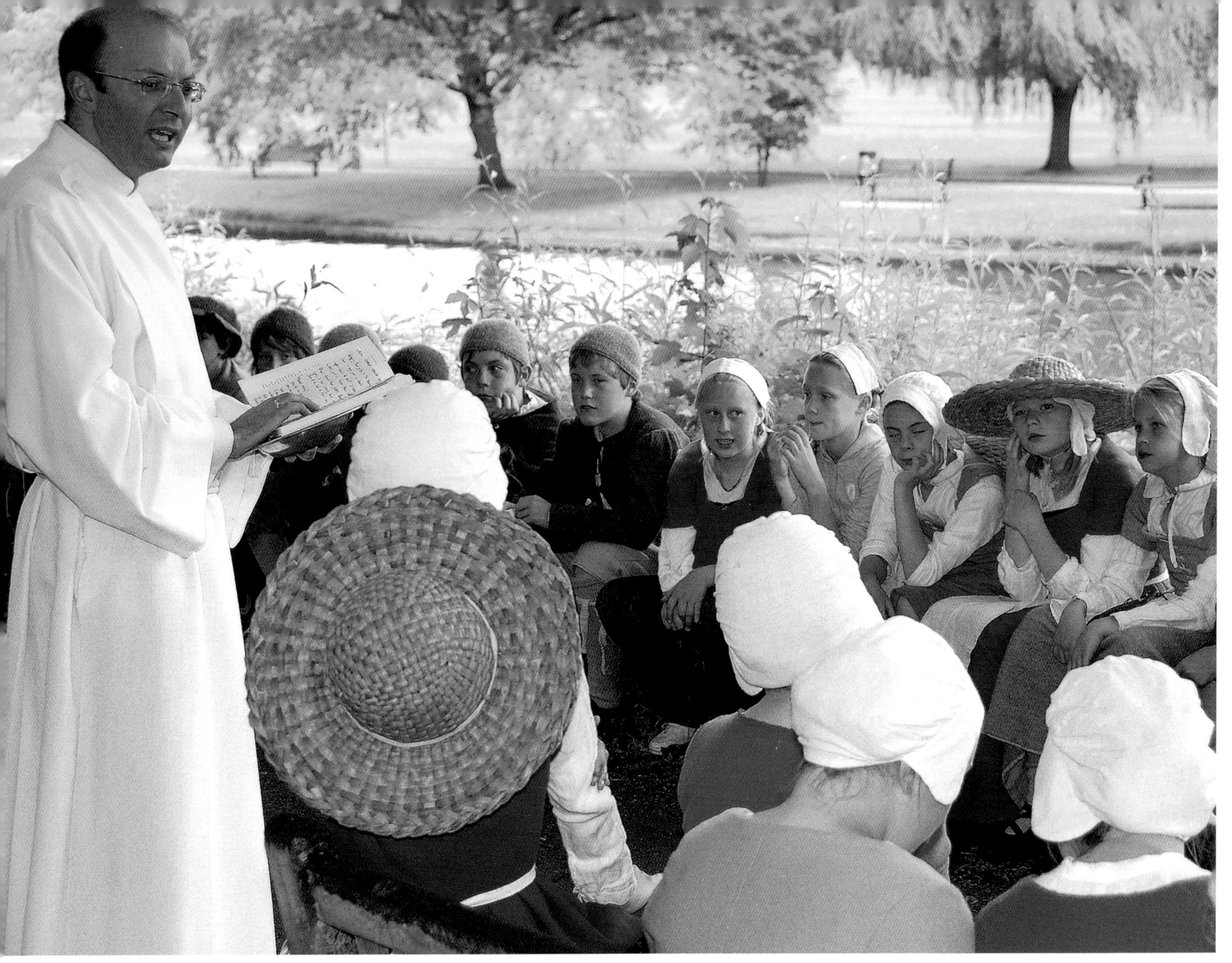

ACTIVITIES FOR CHILDREN

An area at the west end of the nave is set aside for children, and special activities are regularly planned for them. The church also has active links with all the schools in the parish. Jan Craven developed a lay assembly group called 'The Jesus People from Holy Trinity' who lead regular assemblies in the four state primary schools in the parish, and in Welcombe Hills Special School. The new curate and youth minister, Stuart Labran, is also developing imaginative links with the secondary schools and Stratford College.

As part of the 2010 800th anniversary celebrations, there was a week-long series of events called 'Time Travellers', in which groups of primary school children took part in activities based in separate areas around the church, each one set in a different historical period: medieval, Tudor, Victorian and modern. Story-telling, prayers and songs form part of the occasion, and a large candle was lit at the start. With the conclusion of the morning's activities each school lit their own candle from it to take away with them. The final day offered similar activities to children with special needs. The aim was to place the church firmly at the centre of the community, and to encourage the children to focus, through the timeline stretching back into the past and forward into the future, on their place in the long history of the church and the town.

A similar, ongoing initiative is run by the education team at The Shakespeare Birthplace Trust. Called 'Willingly to School', and aimed at primary pupils aged between nine and eleven, it allows the children to take on the identities of real children of their age who lived in Stratford around the time

Elizabethan children

The following are some of the identities today's primary schoolchildren take on when they come 'Willingly to School':

Robert, the son of Roger Green, a miller and brewer, was born in March 1564, a month before Shakespeare, and his family lived in the same street, Henley Street. When he was only a few months old, the terrible plague of that year took six members of his family – three sisters, a brother, an aunt and an uncle.

Gilbert, the son of Thomas Cale, a joiner, lived in Bridge Street. His father was once fined for setting his cart down in a prohibited part of the street – a Tudor parking fine!

Benet Shottelbottel outlived her brother Roger and her two sisters Isabella and Elizabeth, but she herself survived only to the age of twelve.

Emma was the daughter of William Slatter, who married twice and outlived both his wives, but became a poor man and was living in the almshouses when he died.

George, the son of John Perrye, a butcher, lived at 19 Sheep Street. When he grew up he married and had two sons. One died when he was only a baby and the other died a few years later, in the same year that George lost both his father and his mother.

Anna, the daughter of Richard Spooner, a painter, lived in Corn Street (now Chapel Street). She was the only surviving child in her family – her three brothers and four sisters all died young, including twins, Richard and Esther, who died one day apart soon after they were born.

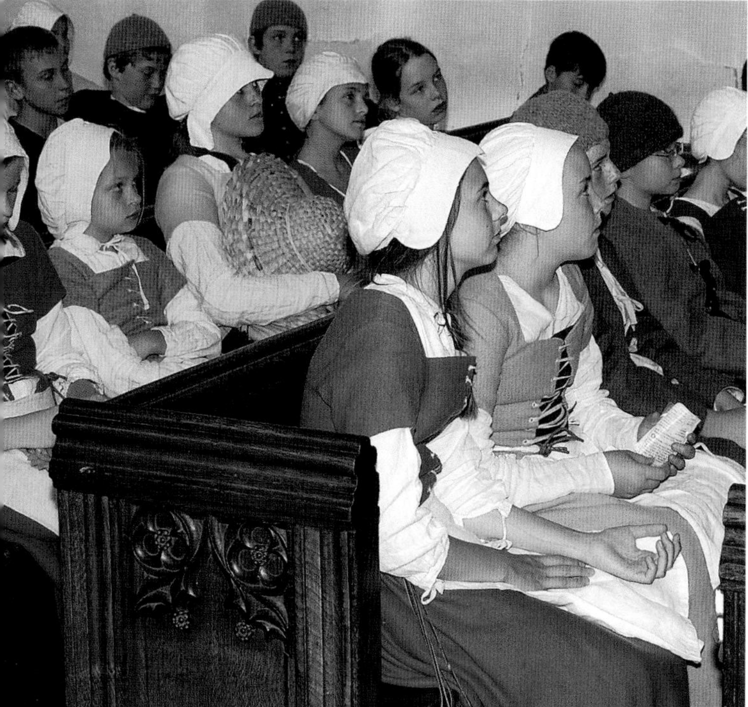

Opposite and below: 'Willingly to School': the children of St Gregory's RC School in Stratford-upon-Avon.

when Shakespeare was a boy, revealed through painstaking research into the records of the time. In addition to using their names for the day, some of the modern children will be able to see where their namesakes once lived and learn something about their parents and siblings (see box). The harshness and brevity of life then is brought all too vividly home to them when they hear about their baby brothers and sisters dying soon after birth or their parents falling victim to the plague.

The day starts with the children getting Tudor-dressed, a process that takes about half an hour as the clothes are beautifully made authentic replicas and require help in putting on – there are no modern fastenings such as zips or Velcro. They keep on their own underwear and shoes, but are all provided with complete costumes made of wool and linen and fastened with laces, ties and buttons. They start with linen smocks and shirts, and then the girls put on their heavy woollen kirtles, fastened with laces down the front and dyed in the authentic colours that would have been available at the time. The boys wear tight doublets (jackets) and baggy breeches, both items fastened to each other by laces at the waist. The children wear long woollen stockings kept up with garters and, on their heads, linen coifs for the girls and woollen 'beanie' caps for the boys. The girls also wear linen aprons, and all the children are reminded that they must do all they can not to soil the expensive and hard-to-clean wool of their clothes.

The girls soon learn to pick up their skirts as they walk through the town to their first lesson of the day, in the petty school in the Guild Chapel, followed by a taste of learning Latin in the Grammar School. Their teacher carries a bundle of canes with which he threatens them if they fail to learn their lessons. In the afternoon there is religious instruction at Holy Trinity church, and then there are Tudor games at Hall's Croft. Authenticity is maintained during the whole day as far as possible: the children are asked to bring lunches that a Tudor child would have eaten – bread, cheese, ham or chicken, an apple or pear and apple juice to drink, but no crisps, bananas, oranges or chocolate!

MEMORIES OF HOLY TRINITY

Worship itself is a pilgrimage

The words above sum up my belief that, regardless of one's age or experience of the Christian faith, there is always something special to be encountered as we make our regular spiritual journey to the altar or to the office of morning or evening prayer. Since retirement from full-time ministry, I have with my wife found Holy Trinity to be a special place for worship and the continuation of service. Martin Gorick, his colleagues and the congregations have been most welcoming and supportive. Indeed it is a great privilege to be – along with other retired clergy – one of the honorary assistant ministers.

This involves giving such pastoral and liturgical assistance as is required, including leading morning prayer in St Peter's Chapel and celebrating Holy Communion at the high altar. When Archbishop Donald Coggan was asked how he intended to spend his retirement he said that, apart from time with his family, he was going to learn how to pray. Just over four years into retirement, I think I know what he meant. The opportunities to officiate at morning prayer in a building so steeped in prayer over the centuries, and with pilgrims and visitors passing by the chapel, enable one to reflect on the spiritual journey we all take and on how, in helping to remember the needs of our parish, town, visitors, diocese and the world-wide church, the voice of prayer is indeed never silent. The times of silence between the daily readings from the Bible also provide rich opportunities for meditation on the word of the Holy Spirit – a regular reminder that holy reading leads to holy listening to God.

Many years ago, I was told of a dedicated parish priest who said that retirement could be difficult because of having to give up service at the altar. Thanks again to Martin's generosity, I share eucharistic and evensong duties on Sundays and weekdays on a rota basis with him and colleagues, thus enabling me to both celebrate and preach. On other occasions, retirement enables me to sit with my wife in church, to go with her to the altar and through the liturgy to be spiritually fed by Martin and colleagues.

I referred above to celebrating at the high altar. To do this so near to the graves of Thomas Balsall and William Shakespeare is a privilege indeed. It enables one to reflect deeply on the spiritual and liturgical developments their own times witnessed and how we may, to quote Archbishop Rowan Williams, '...emerge from the study of the past with some greater fullness of Christian maturity'.

Tony Boyd-Williams

A Catholic mass in Holy Trinity

When Councillor Cyril George Kemp died in January 1979, there was some discussion about the venue for his funeral. For he was a Catholic, and St Gregory's church was undergoing repairs; moreover, the funeral of such a prominent member of the Stratford community – born and bred in Stratford, educated at KES, a past licensee of the Old Red Lion Hotel and a popular mayor of Stratford during the 1960s – was bound to attract a large congregation. As the current mayor, I talked to Canon Peter Barnes and Father Robert Richardson about the possibility of holding the requiem mass for Cyril Kemp at Holy Trinity.

So it came about that, with the glad cooperation of the vicar and churchwardens of Holy Trinity, the first Roman Catholic mass for 440 years, since the Reformation, took place there on February 1 1979. The service was conducted by Father Richardson and Father Vincent Deane, Cyril Kemp's chaplain. St Gregory's church choir was augmented by members of the Stratford Operatic Society, and the readings were given by Father Richardson and myself. The church was very crowded, despite heavy rain, and many of the congregation followed Councillor Kemp's wishes after the service by 'partaking of liquid refreshment' arranged by his executors.

Dr Geoffrey Lees

The stream of tourists wanting to visit the church and see Shakespeare's grave is never ending and the church staff get used to being accosted as they are locking up at the end of the day by people who have arrived too late but who are keen to be let in. Sometimes it is good to relent, and on one occasion when I did so, I was rewarded by meeting someone rather out of the ordinary. I had let in a group of six people and was showing them the chancel when one of the men pointed out an older lady and informed me that she was Mickey Rooney's wife. She was overjoyed at seeing the church and was adamant that Mickey would wish to come at some future time. She insisted that I contact them at the London theatre where he was currently performing. Sadly, the show closed before I was able to do so, so I never met him. He had, of course, a cinematic Shakespeare connection, having played Puck in Max Reinhardt's 1935 film of *A Midsummer Night's Dream*.

On another occasion, the church bursar faced an imploring foreign visitor: 'It has taken me my whole life to get here.' The bursar's deadpan response was, 'Well, you should have started twenty minutes earlier!' **Tim Raistrick**

Microphones have improved the ability of the hard of hearing to enjoy services in church, but they can have their drawbacks, particularly the radio microphone which is clipped onto the robes of the clergy, allowing them to be heard anywhere in the church. Holy Trinity has always been blessed with having a number of retired clergy to assist the full-time ones, and for a number of years one of these was the Right Reverend Vernon Nicholls, the newly retired Bishop of Sodor and Man. After one morning service, the bishop returned to the vestry and, without realising that he had the microphone still switched on, described to another priest the full details of a rather intimate operation he was about to undergo, much to the consternation of some rather innocent female parishioners who heard it all broadcast loudly into the body of the church. **Tim Raistrick**

My connection with Holy Trinity church lies in the fact that, though I now live in Stratford, I went to school in Northwich, Cheshire. My school was Sir John Deane's Grammar School, which had been founded in 1557. Its first master was John Bretchgirdle, who was appointed vicar of Holy Trinity in 1561. His claim to fame is that he baptised William Shakespeare. **Irene Whitley**

My grandfather, William Richard Workman, joined the staff of Holy Trinity church in about 1918 as verger. He had previously served with the 2nd Battalion Grenadier Guards and later joined the Warwickshire County Constabulary. It was while serving with them that he heard gunshots coming from the garden of Masons Croft, Marie Corelli's home, and disarmed the man he found lurking there.

His work at the church included the upkeep of the churchyard, and he gave special attention to the avenue of limes known as the Twelve Apostles. They were pruned annually, and any infected or rotten wood was removed and the holes filled with cement to prevent rainwater creating further damage. The cement filling was still visible when the trees were felled. I became a sponsor for one of the new trees that were planted in 1993/4 to replace the old avenue.

My grandfather worked at Holy Trinity for twenty-five years. On his death the vicar, Canon Noel Prentice, paid tribute to his faithfulness, enthusiasm, loyalty and love of the church, and in special recognition of his long service walked at the front of the funeral cortege from the church to the cemetery.

My father, Percy, and my uncle, Francis, both sang in the choir and my father was also a sidesman. I too sang in the choir as a boy – and one of the advantages was that we were paid. The amount we received depended on attendance, which encouraged a good turnout. We were paid quarterly, and my favourite payment was the one on October 1, which I usually spent at the Mop Fair. **Richard Workman**

Holy Trinity gets visitors from all countries of the world and prides itself on the variety of languages in which it offers the guide sheet. However, even communicating with Americans can, on occasions, prove that a language barrier exists. A verger was once approached by an American woman who asked for the 'comfort room'; as he didn't understand this euphemism for lavatory and assumed she just wanted to rest, he caused much consternation by informing her that she was welcome to use a pew. **Tim Raistrick**

My mother, Monica Mary Pippet, born in 1892, was the daughter of the rector of St Helen's church, Clifford Chambers. She learnt to play the organ at Holy Trinity before becoming organist and choir mistress at St Helen's. She kept up for years with her organ teacher, Mr Bloomer, and was also a lifelong friend of Ursula Bloom. My father, Reverend Thomas Edward Mayo Boultbee, was curate at Holy Trinity from 1921 to 1931 and always remembered 'collecting the daffodils' at Shakespeare's grave on April 23. He later became vicar of Bishopton, where he and my mother married in 1926. He was also priest-in-charge of Shottery and I was born at Shottery parsonage in 1927.

I attended the Croft School, then in Old Town, as a boarder from 1937 to 1947, and regularly went to church at Holy Trinity. I was confirmed and made my first communion there when Canon Prentice was vicar. I well remember the ringing of the church bells, particularly on practice night. I have lived in Australia since the 1960s, but keep up with Stratford news through the *Herald*, which I receive by mail. I am also a life member of the Friends of Shakespeare's Church. **Judith Nedderman**

It is not unusual to have famous faces in the congregation, and one Sunday, I was tipped off that we had the Archbishop of Canterbury sitting in one of the pews. Thinking it was my duty as churchwarden to warn the clergy, and save them the shock of seeing him when they addressed the congregation, I hurried to impart the news in the clergy vestry. However, not wanting to make too much of it, I very discreetly told David Banbury, who was taking the service, that Rowan Williams was there. A fellow priest half overheard the exchange and, thinking that I had said that Rowan Atkinson was in church, convinced David that this was the name I had used. Thus it was that the clergy and servers, excited at the thought of seeing the famous comedy actor in their midst, were ever so slightly disappointed when they discovered it was 'only' the Archbishop of Canterbury. **Tim Raistrick**

Left: The Bishopton Chalice, 1571.

Opposite: Detail of the St George window in the west end of the south aisle.

OUR SPIRITUAL VISION

David Banbury

In the midst of all the activities and events that contribute to the life of Holy Trinity, the central calling of the church is to worship God and make Jesus known in the world. Throughout its history worship has been the primary purpose of the church, although the style and format of that worship have changed over the centuries.

The calling to make Jesus known in the world has been expressed in different ways in different times. In recent years, Holy Trinity has developed a deepening commitment to this challenge, expressed through a renewed emphasis on mission, outreach and church growth within the life of the community.

Holy Trinity's vision statement – 'to be bridge builders bringing God to people and people to God' – expresses the desire of the congregation to reach out both to the people of Stratford and to visitors to the town and church with the good news of God's love and forgiveness. In pursuit of this vision statement, the church has in recent years developed a number of programmes and initiatives, for example the blossoming and expansion of the church's youth work, and the development of an extensive 'Growing Together' programme, designed to help all members of the church community deepen their faith and trust in Christ. And for those outside the church, inquirers' courses are run regularly to help them to explore the Christian faith and consider the life and claims of Jesus. A recent appointment to the clergy team is a director of mission and faith development, with the specific role of helping to facilitate all the aims contained in and expressed through the vision statement.

There are many signs of vigorous new growth and life within Holy Trinity's community – recognised not least through the increased numbers of people who are now regular church members. New churchgoers are always welcome, and are encouraged to become part of the church through events designed to introduce them to the people and activities that make Holy Trinity such a vibrant place.

Our vision is a huge undertaking; but there is ample evidence that the congregation is deeply committed to working towards such a goal.

AFTERWORD: THE COLLEGIATE CHURCH

Martin Gorick

Our vision as a church community at Holy Trinity is to be 'bridge-builders – bringing God to people and people to God through the power of the Spirit and in union with Christ'.

For 800 years now this church has borne witness to the reality of God in the heart of this community. Built on the site of an ancient Saxon monastery, on the banks of the river with its Celtic name of 'Avon', generations have found this to be a holy place.

The exact date of Holy Trinity's foundation is not known, as is often the case with medieval churches that have grown from the foundations of older sacred spaces. We know that key parts of the building date from the 'early years of the thirteenth century' and by long tradition 1210 has been held as its founding date. 2010 has been a good point to take stock and to celebrate the tenacity and vibrancy of the Christian faith in this place, and to pray for God's guidance and blessing for our church and town at this moment in our ongoing history.

We are a 'collegiate' church by foundation, with a 'college' of priests which I am privileged to lead. The Latin name for a member of a college of priests is *pontifex* which means 'bridge-builder'. Priests need to have their feet on the ground and their heads in the clouds; to dream dreams but also to keep grounded and practical as they seek to follow Jesus in whom divinity and humanity are forever entwined. It is our joy to clear the bridge or pathway between God and his people and between people and God. That is the job that we share with all Christians here, for we are *all* called to be bridge-builders wherever we are, as individuals and together as the body of Christ, the church.

Being a 'collegiate' church reminds us that we are all, lay and ordained, called together to be God's priest in this place, calling God's people home and encouraging many more to become part of the great ongoing story of God the Holy Trinity.

Many people come to Holy Trinity looking for Shakespeare. We hope that they leave having found something of God.

The bishop's crook, fashioned in the nineteenth century from wood taken from old pews.

GLOSSARY

AMDG – *Ad maiorem dei gloriam,* to the greater glory of God
aumbry – a cupboard in the wall of a church used to store altar vessels
burgage – tenure of land in a town on a yearly rent
clerestory – a range of high-level windows that bring light into the centre of a church
crocket – decoration in the form of curved or bent foliage
escutcheon – in heraldic terms, a shield displaying a coat of arms
grotesque – a decorative carving; when it incorporates a waterspout it is known as a gargoyle
halfyard – a measure of land
harpy – a bird with a woman's head
hoodmould – a projection above a door or window intended to protect the area below from rainwater, but also used decoratively
messuage – a dwelling house with outbuildings and lands assigned to its use
piscina – a shallow basin, often with a drain, used for washing altar vessels
recusancy – failure to conform to the established religion
reredos – a screen behind an altar
rood – the sculptural representation of the crucifixion
sedilium – a seat for the priest
tympanum – the semicircular or triangular decorative wall surface over an entrance
villein – a medieval peasant who was legally tied to the land he worked on
wyvern – a heraldic beast with a serpent's tail, a dragon's head, wings and two legs

The Latin lines on Shakespeare's monument read

Judicio Pylium, Genio Socratem, Arte Maronem
Terra tegit, populus maeret, Olympus habet

which translate as 'Earth covers, the nation mourns, and heaven holds/a Nestor in counsel, a Socrates in mind, a Virgil in art'.

Nestor was the king of Pylos in southern Greece, well known in Homeric times for his wisdom; Socrates was the Athenian philosopher who taught Plato; and Publius Vergilius Maro was the full name of the Roman poet commonly known as Virgil.

The Shakespeare arms are described in heraldic terms as 'Or, on a bend sable, a tilting spear of the first, point upwards headed argent. Crest, a falcon displayed argent, supporting a spear in pale or'. Thanks to Bill Hicks for the following explanation:

'Or' is heraldic gold, usually rendered as yellow. In this case it refers to the 'field' of the shield, in other words its background colour. A 'bend' is a sloping strip extending across the shield from bottom right to top left and in this case it is coloured 'sable', the heraldic name for black. A 'tilting spear of the first' means a spear of the same colour as the first feature to be mentioned, which is 'or', so the spear is yellow and is placed 'on a bend sable' which means on the black strip. 'Point upwards headed argent' means the tip points towards the upper corner and is coloured 'argent', which is the heraldic name for silver, usually rendered white. The 'crest' sits on top of the shield, and a 'falcon displayed' has its wings spread in the manner of a German eagle. A 'spear in pale or' is yellow and is held in a vertical position.

BRIEF BIBLIOGRAPHY

Baker, Harold, 1908, *The Collegiate Church of Stratford-on-Avon & other buildings of interest in the town and neighbourhood,* 2 edn
Bate, Jonathan, 2008, *Soul of the age: the life, mind and world of William Shakespeare*
Bearman, Robert (ed) 1997, *The history of an English borough*
Bearman, Robert (ed), nd, *Church, chapel and school records – a compilation of all references compiled by Mary Wells and other members of the Holy Trinity congregation,* The Shakespeare Birthplace Trust archives
Bloom, J Harvey, 1902, *Shakespeare's church, otherwise the Collegiate Church of the Holy Trinity of Stratford-upon-Avon*
Bloom, Ursula, 1966, *Rosemary for Stratford-on-Avon*
Dugdale Society, 1921, *Minutes and accounts of the Corporation of Stratford-upon-Avon and other records 1553–1620,* vol 1 1553–1566
Greer, Germaine, 2007, *Shakespeare's wife*
Homer, Bryan, 2005, *Shakespeare's rasher of bacon*
Hughes, Ann, 1997, 'Building a godly town: religious and cultural divisions in Stratford-upon-Avon, 1560–1640, in Bearman 1997, 97–109
Hutchings, L [L H] and Lucy, M [M L], undated but 1896, *An old sanctuary*
Kitcher, Freda, 2006, *Guide to the Collegiate Church of the Holy and Undivided Trinity, Stratford-upon-Avon*
Kitcher, Freda, 2006, *A parson and his parish*
Macdonald, Mairi, 2001/2, '"Not a memorial to Shakespeare, but a place for divine worship": the vicars of Stratford and the Shakespeare phenomenon, 1616–1964', *Warwickshire History,* XI, no 6
Price, Diana, 1997, 'Reconsidering Shakespeare's monument', *The Review of English Studies,* XLVIII(190), 168–81
Wainwright, Patricia, 1989, *The windows of the church of the Most Holy and Undivided Trinity, Stratford-upon-Avon*
Wells, Stanley, 2007, *Is it true what they say about Shakespeare?*
Wheler, Robert Bell, 1806, *The history and antiquities of Stratford*
White, Mary Frances, 1974, reprinted 1991, *Fifteenth-century misericords in the Collegiate Church of the Holy Trinity, Stratford-upon-Avon*
Wood, Michael, 2003, *In search of Shakespeare*
Yorke, Francis, nd, Scrapbook about his work on the church, presented to The Shakespeare Birthplace Trust by his granddaughter

THE SHAKESPEARE BIRTHPLACE TRUST

The Shakespeare Birthplace Trust (reg charity no 209302, www.shakespeare.org.uk) was formed in 1847 to purchase and save Shakespeare's Birthplace. Its charitable activities were much later incorporated by an Act of Parliament: to promote Shakespeare throughout the world, to maintain the five Shakespeare houses 'for the benefit of the nation' and to make available a library, archive and museum collection of Shakespeare-related material. Hundreds of thousands of visitors come to see Shakespeare's Birthplace every year, thousands of students and young people take part in our school and university programmes and our designated national collections are consulted by people from all over the world. We are proud and pleased to endorse *Shakespeare's Church: A Parish for the World*. No pilgrimage to Stratford-upon-Avon would be truly complete without visiting Shakespeare's monument and grave in the church where he and his family worshipped, as well as his birthplace, and taking a moment to recognise what his friend Ben Jonson referred to as 'what he hath left us'. Millions of people also thank God for him.

Professor Stanley Wells CBE, Chairman of the Shakespeare Birthplace Trust, carries the wreath to Shakespeare's grave during the annual birthday procession.

SUBSCRIBERS

This book has been made possible through the generosity of the following subscribers.

Robert and Judith Amies
Sir Eric and Lady Anderson
Mary and Michael Anderson
Sally Armitage
Wendy Ashley
Peter and Gillian Ashley-Smith
Alexandra and Guy Attwater
Margaret Austen
Ann Baer
Peggie and Donald Baker
Frank and Ivy Ballard
Ruth Barbour
Clive Barnes
David Barnes
Dr D J Bartlett
Margaret Bartlett
Harry Sebastian Bate
Mr E Beckett
Mr and Mrs Bellamy
Mr and Mrs A P Bird
Miss Gabrielle Blackstock
Sue Blackwell
Mrs Anne J Blair
Andrea Blood
Donatella Bonicelli
Tony and Glenda Boyd-Williams
Brian and Hazel Brazier
Geoff and Heather Bridgewater
M E Briggs
Charlie Brooks
Derek Brownbridge
John and Cilla Burgess
John Burt
Linda Butland
Patricia Butt
Mrs C Campbell
Mr J D G Cashin
Jill and Ray Castle
Anne Charlton
Dr Philip Cheshire
Right Reverend Dr Christopher Cocksworth
Dr Michael Coigley
Ian John Cole
Judith Coleman
Sarah Collins
Mildred J Colvin
Dr Ann Jennalie Cook
Elsie Cooper
Graham E Cooper
In memory of Stella Cornford
Sarah and Luned Corser
Christine Cottrell
Susan Courth
Mrs Mary Cox
Richard and Ann Coxon
Liz Crane
Denise Creamer
The Crimp Family
Chris Crowcroft
Kathleen and Michael Culverwell
Mr D W Curtis
Michelle and Simon Dale
Douglas Daniel
Ann Daniels
Catherine Davies
Mrs Pauline Day
Jeffery Dench and Ann Curtis
Mrs Kari Dill
Peter Dingley
Jennie Dobson
William Dodsworth
Dawn Dollman
Judith and Norman Dorricott
Tom Drake
Sir William Dugdale
Eileen and Ray Dunn
Roger Brien Dunn
Elaine and Tom Durance
Robyn Durie
Gillian L Dyer
Beryl F Dyke
Jill Edmonds
Christopher and Pauline Edmondson
Kathleen Edmondson
Helen Edwards
Margaret Edwards
Mr and Mrs Richard Edwards
The Ellam Family
Charles Elmy
Maureen Elton
Jane M Epstein
Squadron Leader Beryl E Escott
Jeremy J Evans
Mr and Mrs J Farrar
Chris Fellows
Rachel M Field
Sir Brian and Lady Follett
G R and J P Forbes
Mrs Vida Forrest
Neville Fox
Paul J D Fulham JP
Donald Gardner
Robert and Elizabeth Gifford
Deidre Gillam
Mrs R F Goode
Lionel Gorick MBE
The Gorick Family
Colin and Gabrielle Gott
The Gray Family: John, Sally, Alison and Richard
Dr Lawrence Green and Mrs Therese Green

Mrs S Greenway
J A Greenwood
Peter Gregory-Hood
Mrs Anne Grey
Kent Hägglund
Mr and Mrs Leslie Hamilton
Mr and Mrs D J Hammond
Mrs M C Hanney
Mrs Brenda Harding
David Hargreaves
Mrs Jean Harper
Andrew Harris
Barbara C Harris
Margaret Ann Harris
Brian G Harrison
Molly Harrison
Francis Nicholas Hatfield
Wendy Hefford
Ian and Jennifer Heggie
Lyndon and Margaret Hellier
Mary Helyar
Dr and Mrs John Henderson
W R G Hicks
David Vincent Hird
S Donald Holdsworth
John Burman Holtom
Graham and Lilian Hopkins
Paul and Margaret Hopkins
Robert and Jane Hornby
Mrs Pamela M Howes
Robert Terry Hoyle
G H and P A Hubbard
Heather Hughes
Jemima Daisy Rosamond Huish
Brenda E Humby
Sasha John Hurley
John Ilott
Miss W Mary James
Mr David R E Jenson
Margaret Olwen Jones
Michele Lynn Kaminski
Barbara and Barry Keeling
Clive and Janet Kempton
C J Kennedy
John Kilby
Mrs M J Kingston
Arthur F Kinney
Tetsuo Kishi
Freda Kitcher
Seiei Kobayashi
Professor and Mrs R D Langman
Mrs D Laurens
Jean and Derek Lawrance
Dr Geoffrey Lees
James Leonard
Diana Letts
Jill Levenson
José I L Lewis
Sheila Lindsay
David Lloyd
Eleanor Grace Hannah Lofthouse
Dr William B Long
Joyce Loveless
Mrs Josephine Lytton
Duncan M Macleay
Victoria and Craig Mahon
Sheila Mahoney
Ian Martin
Susan Martin
C and J McDowall
William McFarland
Alan P McLean
Henry Meadows
Janet Mellor
Mrs Kathleen Messent
Val and Mike Milburn
Michael and Sheila Mills
Dr Jonathan Milton
Eden Mollway
Tim and Iwona Moore-Bridger
M J Moran
Ann Morgan
Ann Morris
Caroline Mosey
Richard Mullings
Charlotte Mulryne
Edward Mulryne
Ronnie and Eithne Mulryne
Marga Munkelt
D E Murray
Judith M Nedderman
M P Needham-Bennett
Miss P Newbury
Carol Hamilton Newhouse
Dana Christopher Newhouse
Hollie and Paul Nielsen
Tadaaki Noguchi
Ronald F Offord
Becky Ormrod
Helen Ormrod
Margaret and David Ormrod
Sheonagh and Jon Ormrod
Ruth Örs
Sir John Owen
Diana Owen
Bryan and Margaret Palin
John Parkes
Kath Parrington
Terry Parris
Carl E Parrish Jr
Keith Payne
Ray Pedlingham
Catherine Penn
Betty Percival
Martin Perkins
Mary and David Phillips
Lavinia Phipps

Tim Piggott-Smith
Patrick Pilton
Jenny Plenderleith
Reverend and Mrs Robert J Powell
David and Jennifer Prescott
John Gwilym Price
Margaret Eileen Price
Dorothy Raistrick
Tim Raistrick
Martin Rawbone
Susan Robinson
George Malcom Rooks
Dryden Rooney
Emily Carol Russell
Ray and Margaret Russell
Ursula Russell
Beryl C Sainsbury
David A Scruton
Gwen Sedgwick
Shakespeare Club of Western Australia
Marion Shaw
Freya Alice Simpson
Louise and Angus Simpson
Rowan Connor Simpson
D A and S Sladden
Mrs Ann Smart
Ralph H Smith
Edward Spinks Esq
The late Gordon Leslie Spinks
George Sprawson, in memory of Joan
Daphne and Graham Stanbridge
P and J Standing
Audrey Stone
Bryan Stoten
Susan Strickland
Mrs W Strophair
John A Styler
S A Styles
Laurence Kent Sweeney
Lucy R Sweet
Lynette J Sweet
George Sykes
Mayumi Tamura
Neville Tarratt
Hazel and Chris Tattersall
Peggy Tearne
Amelia and Henry Teehan
Valerie Thompson
Heather M Thomson
Greig Tillotson
Miyoko Tokioka
John E Toll
Mrs Mary Tomlinson-Jones
Carol Eden Tubb
Reverend D F Tunbridge
Charles Twigger
Kara Ukolowicz
Margaret Rowena Usmar
Susan E Vaughton
Jo Vincent
Margaret Wade
Mrs Josephine Walker
Patricia Clayson and Alan Wall
Helen M Wallace
Wendy Warnken and Stephen Johnson
Helen and Mike Warrillow
Stella Webley
Wellington Shakespeare Society, New Zealand
Greg and Mary Wells
Professor Stanley Wells CBE
Anthony Van West
Lt Col G A A R West
Frances and David Westcott
Mr and Mrs Michael Westwood
John White
Irene Whitley
Norma Whittard
Reverend and Mrs Graham Wilcox
James H Willetts
A B Williams
Eric and Adele Wills
Betty Wilson
Alan Alfred Wincote
Tony Jose Winters
Pat Wood
Anthony Woollard
R Workman
John Wright
Barry Wylam
Professor Junko Yamazaki
Miss Doreen Yellow
Mrs P M Young

INDEX OF NAMES

Italics denotes artist or image
Bold denotes contributor